D1125385

PRAISE FOR THE P...

THE TWO TRILLION DOLLAR MELTDOWN

A *New York Times* bestseller
A *Wall Street Journal* bestseller

"Few writers are as good as Morris at making financial arcana understandable and even fascinating."
—Floyd Norris, *New York Times Book Review*

"[*The Trillion Dollar Meltdown*] is an absolutely excellent narrative of the horror that we have in the credit markets right now. It's a wonderful explanation of how it happened and why it's so rotten, and why it will take a long time to unwind."
—Paul Steiger, editor-in-chief, ProPublica, and former managing editor, *The Wall Street Journal*

"[A] shrewd primer.... [Morris] writes with tight clarity and blistering pace."
—James Pressley, *Bloomberg News*

"Morris, a former banker, [earned] rock-solid status as a predictor of the crash. He homes in on the complexity and the paradoxical unpredictability of these financial instruments, which were supposed to manage risk and ended up magnifying it."
—*New Yorker*

"Morris provides a comprehensive and jargon-free description of the hideously complex financial securities that have brought the credit system to collapse. It is a remarkable story."
—*Sunday Times* (London)

"Charles Morris provides an excellent and timely analysis of the origins, causes, and turbo-charged financial engineering that allowed cheap and excessive debt to create a bloated financial system."
—Satyajit Das, author of *Traders, Guns & Money: Knowns & Unknowns in the Dazzling World of Derivatives*

"Amid the hyperbole, several financial-scare books stand out for their high credibility and low hysteria. *The Trillion Dollar Meltdown* by Charles R. Morris ... avoid[s] the wild predictions of mass economic destruction, instead giving thoughtful, if alarming, histories and analyses of how we got into the mess we're in today."

—Susan Antilla, *Bloomberg News*

"Charles Morris, author of *The Trillion Dollar Meltdown*, isn't one for sugarcoating. His analysis is dour and grim, but certainly not dull. And when read against a backdrop of an ever-weaker economy, increasingly anxious economists, and a stream of gloomy predictions, it can be downright scary. Morris serves up a sharp, thought-provoking historical wrap-up of the U.S. economy and its markets, along with clear scrutiny of today's economic woes."

—*USA Today*

"My favorite single book account [of the subprime crisis]."

—Business & Economics Correspondent
Adam Davidson, NPR's "Planet Money"

"Millions of words have been written about the ongoing financial disaster largely caused by the subprime mortgage mess. But the most concise and easiest to understand handbook on the issue is almost certainly Charles R. Morris' *The Trillion Dollar Meltdown: Easy Money, High Rollers, and the Great Credit Crash*."

—Robert Bryce, *The Texas Observer*

"[A] masterful and sobering book."

—Commonweal

"To better understand how the world economy has been pushed to the brink and what the post-crash political/economic environment might eventually look like, this book provides both insight and a possible peek into our future."

—Larry Cox, *Tucson Citizen*

"Will provide some important background that will help decipher the meaning behind today's gloomy financial headlines. For those who wonder 'Why?', here's a place to get some answers!"

—*Watsonville (CA) Register-Pajaronian*

THE TWO TRILLION DOLLAR
MELTDOWN

EASY MONEY, HIGH ROLLERS,

AND THE GREAT CREDIT CRASH

CHARLES R. MORRIS

PUBLICAFFAIRS
NEW YORK

Copyright © 2008 by Charles R. Morris.

Hardcover published as *The Trillion Dollar Meltdown* in 2008.

Published in the United States by PublicAffairs™, a member of the Perseus Books Group.

All rights reserved.

Printed in the United States of America.

No part of this book may be reproduced in any manner whatsoever without written permission except in the case of brief quotations embodied in critical articles and reviews. For information, address PublicAffairs, 250 West 57th Street, Suite 1321, New York, NY 10107. PublicAffairs books are available at special discounts for bulk purchases in the U.S. by corporations, institutions, and other organizations. For more information, please contact the Special Markets Department at the Perseus Books Group, 2300 Chestnut Street, Suite 200, Philadelphia, PA, 19103, call (800) 810-4145 ext. 5000, or email special.markets@perseusbooks.com.

The Library of Congress catalogued the hardcover edition as follows:
Morris, Charles R.
    The trillion-dollar meltdown : easy money, high rollers, and the great credit crash / Charles R. Morris. — 1st ed.
        p. cm.
    Includes bibliographical references and index.
    ISBN 978-1-58648-563-4 (hbk.)
    ISBN 978-1-58648-691-4 (pbk.)
    1. Capital market—United States. 2. Finance—United States.
3. Financial crises—United States. I. Title.

HG4910.M667 2008
332'.04150973—dc22

2007048207

First Edition

10 9 8 7 6 5 4 3 2 1

For Charlie-chan

CONTENTS

FOREWORD TO
THE PAPERBACK EDITION

Sometime in October 2008, markets finally "got it." The world was stuck in a vicious credit crunch and teetering on the brink of a frightening recession. Stock markets plunged everywhere, currencies whipsawed violently, interbank lending seized up. Governments poured out trillions in loans, equity infusions, and bailouts, while credit markets stayed obstinately stuck on "Closed." The U.S. Federal Reserve Bank, in an unprecedented, and unilateral, expansion of its powers, pumped out $1.1 trillion in new lending in about six weeks—to banks, broker-dealers, a big insurer, commercial paper issuers, and money market funds.

A $700 billion bank bailout bill was rammed through the American Congress on the promise that it would get at "the root cause" of the crisis by buying up toxic assets from banks' books. European governments, led by Great Britain, trumped

the American bailout with the much more focused strategem
of equity infusions directly into the banks. Treasury Secretary
Henry Paulson, a former president of Goldman Sachs and
arch-antagonist of interventional government, was grudg-
ingly forced to follow suit, only to find the queue of petition-
ers lengthening by the day—not just banks, but insurance
companies, state governments, and automobile companies.
There was even talk of lending to hedge funds.

For the first time, finance ministers realized how deeply
the lethal new financial instruments from America had pene-
trated global investment portfolios; and how far their own
banks, especially in Europe, had gone in emulating the American giants. Europe's hope that it could "de-couple" its economy from America's vanished, as the continent slid toward
negative growth. The petrostates—Russia, Venezuela, Iran,
and the Arab states—who had linked their spending to the
infinite gluttony of the American consumer, stared into the
abyss. Even economies—like those of Korea, Taiwan, and
Brazil—that had maintained strong reserves and mostly
sound practices were staggered in the gusts. Iceland, which
had taken a riskier path, went bankrupt.

The global crisis, however, was indeed made in America,
despite the sins of its imitators and fellow travelers. At its
core, it was a crisis of the classic "Argentinean" variety—a
debt-fed party, marked by a consumer binge on imported
goods, and the strutting of an ostentatious new class of super-
rich, who had invented nothing and built nothing, except in-
tricate chains of paper claims that duller people mistook for
wealth. This was the same America, of course, that had
preached the strait-laced "Washington consensus"—increase

savings, balance budgets, run trade surpluses—in the wake of the Latin American and Asian crises of the 1980s and 1990s.

This new edition of the book goes to press in the early months of Year Two of the Great Credit Crunch. Since the first edition was completed in November 2007, when the crash was still in its early stages, a brief summary of Year One is in order.

From today's perspective, the late spring of 2007 seems like a different era. American financial markets were unusually sunny; consumer spending was growing strongly; the market for investment-grade credit was booming; and the premiums demanded to invest in riskier forms of debt were at an all-time low. The S&P 500 jumped more than 9 percent just from March through May.

A first seismic quiver came in mid-June when it was disclosed that two Bear Stearns mortgage hedge funds could not meet margin calls. A Moody's downgrade had reduced the value of certain of their investment-grade "subprime" mortgage-based bonds. The fund sold some of its bonds to raise money, but most of the rest, it turned out, were not salable at any price. The value of all subprime-related debt tumbled. The experience was frightening, but cooler heads reminded the world that subprime mortgages were a small market and the problem was "contained."

Then subprime-related problems began to pop up all around the world. A $900 million London hedge fund closed its door. There was a run on a big London mortgage lender. German and Swiss banks announced large writeoffs. In August, the

Federal Reserve and the European Central Bank flooded their economies with fresh money.

Alarming new revelations poured out. Big banks, especially Citigroup, it seemed, held hundreds of billions of long-term loans in mysterious off-balance sheet entities called SIVs that they financed in the short-term commercial paper market. The shock of the disclosure brought interbank lending to a grinding halt. On top of that, banks were sitting on hundreds of billions in "bridge loan" commitments to finance highly-leveraged private equity company buyouts. But the banks had assumed that they would be able to sell off those loans into the same markets that were now choking on subprime paper. Banks tried to back out of the deals. Legal papers flew.

The Federal Reserve rode to the rescue, with an aggressive cut in the base short-term lending rate in September and an-other in October. Hosannahs were sung to Ben S. Bernanke—then newly installed as Fed chairman—the stock market leaped, and credit markets jittered back to life.

The losses disclosed in the October bank earnings releases were shocking—some $20 billion in asset writedowns, with about half of them at Merrill Lynch and Citi—but the mar-kets actually rose in relief that the bad news was finally out. Relief turned to horror just days later, when both Merrill and Citi acknowledged that they had grossly underestimated their losses. Even more alarming, in November, Gary Crittenden, the Citigroup CFO, told analysts that he did not know how to value the complex new instruments at the heart of Citi's problems.

The October fiasco set the pattern for subsequent quarters. The losses at the major banks kept growing, as did uncertainty about the real value of bank assets. CEOs were fired, often expensively. (Stan O'Neal, ousted as CEO of Merrill, was paid more than $200 million from 2006 through the fall of 2007.) Federal Reserve interventions were ever more extreme. In December, the Fed tried to re-liquefy banks by exchanging Treasuries for some of their riskier credit instruments. Through the spring, it steadily expanded the instruments it would accept as collateral and the range of financial companies it would lend to, but the effects of its successive interventions steadily dwindled. Nervous markets continually teetered on the edge of panic.

The first big bank to topple was Bear Stearns, in March 2008. Like all the investment banks, its trading books were highly leveraged and dependent on short-term financing. As doubts grew about the value of its large and opaque mortgage portfolio (it could be valued only by Bear's internal models) lenders finally refused to roll over its credit lines. Bankruptcy was avoided only by a forced merger with JP Morgan.

The dominos kept falling. Countrywide Financial, the biggest American mortgage lender, was rescued by Bank of America in May. In August, shockingly, Fannie Mae and Freddie Mac, the giant mortgage lenders with some $5 trillion in home loans, were taken over by the government.

Next on the chopping block was Lehman Bros., which had long been suspected of excessively optimistic financial statements. Lehman was bigger than Bear, but arguably in worse shape, and Paulson and Bernanke had long been pressing it to bring in more equity. But the longtime Lehman CEO, Richard Fuld, delayed and delayed until he was finally forced to ask for government help. Paulson decided to draw a line in the sand. With no merger prospects, Lehman filed for bankruptcy on September 15.

The same weekend that Lehman was allowed to go down, the insurance giant AIG, which ran a high-risk trading operation out of its central office, petitioned the Fed for a large "temporary" loan and was summarily rejected—it was not even a bank. But AIG was the guarantor on $300 billion of American mortgage-backed CDOs held by European banks, worth at best fifty cents on the dollar. Those guarantees would fail if AIG did, forcing European banks to write off some $150 billion in assets. Finance ministry telephone lines crackled, and on Monday night, Paulson capitulated, with an $85 billion loan (which has now grown to $123 billion) on very harsh terms.

Merrill saw the handwriting on the wall and executed a quick midnight elopement with Bank of America. That week, both Morgan Stanley and the once-invincible Goldman Sachs petitioned the Fed to convert to full Federal Reserve Bank status, trading their relative freedom from regulation for the assurance of quick aid in a crisis.

The Lehman failure, however, was a watershed. Not even Paulson or Bernanke suspected how deeply its securities were marbled through the world financial system. Money market mutual funds are a major source of short-term liquidity to banks, and one of the biggest of them all, the Reserve Fund—with $65 billion in Lehman paper—announced that it had "broken the buck." It could not return the sacrosanct $1 a share to investors. All money market funds immediately pulled back their bank lines, triggering a global liquidity crisis.

As panic spread through world markets, Paulson and Bernanke announced their $700 billion bailout plan, at that stage nothing more than a semi-hatched three-page memo. Almost all European governments, led by Great Britain's prime minister, Gordon Brown, came into the markets in force. By November, there was a scarcely a major bank on the continent that had not received a large infusion of taxpayer cash, while the list of American banks with the federal government as their partner was growing almost by the day.

Yet as of this writing, the sickening stock market downdrafts continue, and credit markets remain semicatatonic. The gut-freezing comprehension is finally taking hold that this is not really, at the end of the day, just a banking phenomenon. America's problems, and therefore the world's, go much deeper than that.

Some simple math tells the story. Starting in the late 1990s, the share of personal consumption in GDP grew from a long-term average of about 66 percent all the way to 72 percent in early 2007—the highest level ever, anywhere. At the same time our trade deficit grew from about 1.3 percent of GDP in the mid–1990s to an average of 4.8 percent of GDP in the 2000s. The increase in spending was mostly fueled by borrowing, mostly against houses.

From 2000 through 2007, home equity withdrawals for personal consumption, making payments on credit cards and other consumer debt, and refurbishing homes totaled about $2.8 trillion, a huge swathe of economic activity. All together, it was equal to about 4 percent of disposable personal incomes. With the collapse of home prices, of course, that finance has all but disappeared.

The flood of credit was pumped out by a brand-new credit turbine—the "shadow banking system," hedge funds, investment banks, off-balance-sheet conduits, and the like. By early 2007, according to the Federal Reserve Bank of New York, the shadow banks' lending book was bigger than the entire traditional banking sector. (They didn't lend directly to homeowners, but bought up loans in huge volumes from mortgage-banker intermediaries.)

The current bailouts perpetuate a standard misconception of the credit bubble—that we have a *liquidity* problem, rather than a *solvency* problem. It's a crucial distinction. A couple of examples illustrate the difference.

Before the development of grain futures markets in the 1870s, American farmers had limited access to capital, and merchants took great risk in buying grain and shipping it overseas. But once future deliveries could be sold for cash, a fire hose of investment poured into new grain-belt "factory farms," and turned America into a Saudi Arabia of food. Farmers and grain merchants had a *liquidity* problem that was brilliantly solved by financial markets.

Now consider the famous, if possibly legendary, tulip bulb mania in seventeenth-century Holland. As bulb prices skyrocketed, traders took massive risks leveraging up their bulb holdings until someone realized that tulip bulbs are, after all, just a kind of onion. Prices collapsed almost overnight. No amount of lending could have restored the old tulip bulb prices, since onions, at bottom, aren't worth much. The story of the tulip bulbs is a parable of *insolvency*, not illiquidity. And today's housing debt problems, unfortunately, look rather like tulip bulbs.

Over the long term, the appreciation in home prices is about 1 percent a year faster than the rate of inflation, roughly tracking the growth in real incomes. But from 2000 through 2006, when inflation was quite low, major-market home prices jumped by more than 14 percent a year—the fastest prolonged price increase ever—although without any obvious demographic reason. It both attracted, and was prompted by, a flood of finance that made it very easy to buy homes at low interest rates with little or no money down.

Buy a home with 5 percent down, watch it appreciate at 10 percent net of interest costs for three years, and you've recovered your equity investment sevenfold. Buy it at 1 percent down, which was fairly standard, and you've made more than thirty times your equity. In America's efficient capital markets, home values quickly jumped to reflect the present value of the potential capital gains, rather than a steady-state price that a homebuyer could finance from current income on normal lending terms.

Super-efficient financiers allowed you to tap into the new fountains of housing credit without even buying or selling a house—just leverage up the house you already owned. Banks were happy to send you a large bolus of cash for a claim on your home's unrealized value. It was the same as selling a tulip bulb future.

It is impossible to exaggerate the sheer idiocy of the financial machinery of the 2000s. To start with, leverage is extremely high—in the shadow banking world, often as much as 100 to 1. Moreover, the favored instruments, such as collateralized debt obligations (CDOs), are highly illiquid, or hard to sell in a pinch. Even worse, the preferred method for financing positions is in overnight and other short-term money markets, so there are horrendous asset-liability mismatches. Then those highly leveraged, illiquid, short-term–funded CDOs and similar securities are built from securities that themselves carry a high risk of default, primarily sub-prime and so-called "Alt-A," or undocumented, mortgages. Finally, a new class of arcane credit derivatives, completely outside the purview of regulators, ensures that almost all bank portfolios are "tightly coupled" as engineers say, so failures in any part of the system will quickly propagate through the rest. An evil genie could not have designed a structure more prone to disaster.

The focus on high-risk mortgages is especially revealing. Easy money policies at the Fed pushed the yield on prime mortgages so low that banks couldn't build fee-generating CDOs with the kind of yield investors were looking for. So they focused on riskier and riskier loans, even competing to buy up subprime lenders to ensure a flow of product. By 2006, high-risk mortgages accounted for about 40 percent of all mortgage originations. Similar phenomena occurred on a somewhat smaller scale in highly leveraged corporate takeovers, commercial real estate, and auto loans—all of them, to a greater or lesser degree, the financial equivalent of tulip bulb futures.

If the scale of the irresponsibility is staggering, it was in pursuit of equally staggering profits. Data compiled by the Commerce Department show that the financial sector claimed 41 percent of all corporate profits in 2007. The irresponsibility of the financial sector was matched by that of its regulators. The reason that all developed nations regulate their financial sectors is precisely because very highly leveraged players can make huge profits by risking other people's money. When their risks turn out badly, however, the costs tend to fall back to the public, as amply demonstrated by the events of the last several months. Uniquely, the United States adopted a pronounced hands-off attitude toward the financial sector throughout the 2000s, ensuring that taxpayers would eventually reap the whirlwind.

In the first edition of this book, I estimated that the losses to the banking and other investment sectors would be at least $1 trillion, specifying that if the deleveraging is disorderly, the losses could be double or triple that amount. We now seem to be in the midst of a disorderly deleveraging. The highly leveraged players in the shadow banking world, like the hedge funds, are caught in a forced deleveraging as banks pull their margin lending lines and insist on greater collateral against high-risk positions. Deleveraging feeds panic as forced sales drive down prices.

Just through October 2008, large publicly-traded financial institutions reported nearly $700 billion in losses. That number, of course, excludes losses in hedge funds, pension funds, and other investors that must be at least as large. Since the Paulson/Bernanke bailout plan implicitly assumes a continuing stream of bank losses on roughly the same scale for the foreseeable future, the likely losses are now $2 trillion or even more. Indeed, the actual or committed public cash infusions to the banks, including toxic assets "temporarily" absorbed by the Federal Reserve, the multiple bailouts, and the Paulson/Bernanke plan are now—by themselves— close to $2 trillion.

There are reports that cash-hoarding at banks is obstructing normal financing for payrolls and inventories at healthy companies. That is a classic liquidity problem, and the government's equity infusions into banks will be helpful in easing it. But the government can't arrest the fall in housing prices and other misvalued assets until they return to levels consistent with the cash flow and incomes of their borrowers. By most estimates, housing prices still have 10–20 percent more to fall, and the same arithmetic is at work in high-risk corporate bonds, leveraged loans, and commercial mortgages. Solvency issues, that is, still dominate.

The sad reality is that there is no easy way out. For about a decade now, we have had a false prosperity based on a huge water-wheel of money, fueling a debt-financed, import-driven consumer binge. Personal savings rates have dropped to zero, and the world is flooded with dollars. The new dollar-lakes from the Paulson/Bernanke rescue efforts just put us deeper underwater.

Now it's time that we take the same harsh measures we have long preached to other countries. Re-energizing consumer borrowing and spending with cheap money is exactly the wrong prescription. Consumption has to fall, by at least 4–5 percent of GDP, and the money has to be shifted to savings and investment. The hypertrophied financial sector has to shrink drastically. And we have to run down the huge overhang of dollar-based debt by producing more than we buy for the first time in a long time—in effect, by working harder and living poorer.

America is a resilient country, and will prosper again. But the shifts are of such a scale that they cannot be accomplished without a tough recession—and the sooner we get it over with the better. The precedent most on point is Paul Volcker's achievement in reversing skyrocketing consumer prices in the wake of the Great Inflation of the 1970s. It required engineering one of the nastiest recessions on record in 1979–1981, but cleared the ground for twenty years of solid growth. The alternative is a Japanese-style stagnation that could stretch on for a decade or more. By piling on yet more trillions in foreign claims on the United States, the Paulson/Bernanke therapies are making the ultimate tab grow higher.

Unfortunately, there may be no way to repair the damage to America's greatest financial asset of all—the global trust in our financial markets, which have long been a magnet for world capital flows.

The German finance minister, Peer Steinbrück, recently forecast that the American crisis is the beginning of the end of its status as the world's financial superpower. The United States, he said, "is the clear origin and focal point of the crisis . . . spreading through the world like a poisonous oil spill."

He's right on both counts, and it's a shame. During the years of American financial supremacy, dating from the Marshall Plan days, it has been a force for much good, although prone to periodic episodes of irresponsibility. The last decade, however, may rank as the most destructive of all, and

both America and the world will pay the price for a long
time to come.

I wrote this book to tell the story of the credit crisis as briefly
and crisply as I can. I walk the reader through the instruments involved, how they work, and how they are abused. I
untangle—as far as possible—what the outstandings are, why
they are shaky, and build up to the probable loss scenarios
and unwinding scenarios I just described.

In the first two chapters, I recreate the context for the
2000s credit bubble. A long cycle of liberal government-
centric policy-making led to the Great Inflation of the 1970s,
the failed attempts at price controls, and Paul Volcker's great
success in arresting the collapse.

The watershed presidential election of 1980 brought free-
market "Chicago School" ideology to Washington, and with
it financial deregulation and, in the domestic arena, a steady
trimming back of the power of centralized government. The
scorched-earth reconstruction of our bloated post-war "old-
boy" big-company corporate establishment in the first half of
the 1980s was an essential precondition for the restoration of
American competitiveness and the "Goldilocks" economy of
the 1990s.

The prolonged financial boom, however, carried the seeds
of its own destruction. In Chapter 3, I trace three critical
developments of the 1980s and the 1990s—the birth of
"structured finance," the great expansion of derivatives markets, and the mathematization of trading—that flowed together to create the great credit bubble. Chapter 4 delves

further into the arithmetic, the instruments, and the mechanics of the credit bubble, and the crucial enabling role of monetary authorities, especially in America. Chapter 5 focuses on the debasement of the dollar, the huge dollar assets accumulated by some of the world's most unsavory governments, the rise of "Sovereign Wealth Funds," and the humiliations of selling off the family jewels to pay the interest on our past excesses. Finally, in Chapter 6, "The Great Unwinding," I pull together the instruments at risk, lay out the numbers involved, and play through likely unwinding scenarios.

In Chapter 7, I assess some of the broader financial and macroeconomic trends that fed into the bubble, while finally, in Chapter 8, I examine some of the policy responses available to Barack Obama's new administration.

I've always been impressed with a cyclical theory of American politics associated with the senior Arthur Schlesinger—that the political/economic consensus tends to swing between liberal and conservative cycles in roughly twenty-five to thirty-year arcs. In the early days of a cycle the new ways of thinking are like a fresh breeze that blows away the mythologies of the past. Inevitably, through a kind of Gresham's law of incumbency, breezes become doldrums, and leaders get trapped in mythologies of their own. Liberal cycles inevitably succumb to the corruptions of power, conservative cycles to the corruptions of money.

The current conservative, free-market, cycle that commenced with the Reagan presidency, with all its achievements, seems to have long since foundered in the oily seas of gross excess. If nothing else, a restoration of reasonable financial regulation is imperative.

———

Special thanks to Peter Osnos of PublicAffairs. I started working on this book in January 2007, in the expectation of a crash in mid–2008 or so. When events started to catch up to my drafts, he greatly expedited the publishing process, as only Peter can do. My appreciation also to Susan Weinberg and Lindsay Jones at PublicAffairs, who were sharp readers and critics, and had a great deal to do with my being able to stay on schedule; and to Melissa Raymond for her sure production hand. Tim Seldes, my long-time agent at Russell & Volkening, was his usual wise self.

Special thanks also to Nouriel Roubini, of Roubini Global Economics, who was onto this story from the beginning, and who gave me free access to his unmatchable trove of sources; to George Soros for an extended tutorial on currency economics; and to Satyajit Das, who's written most of the textbooks on credit derivatives and structured finance. Since I contacted Das out of the blue one day, he's been a font of technical information and a great sounding board.

I made substantial impositions on friends and acquaintances in the structured finance industry to deepen my understanding of market mechanics and risks. They did me a favor, and I'm returning it by not thanking them by name. I was also the beneficiary of some terrific reporting on the credit bubble in the financial press. So thanks to Serena Ng at *The Wall Street Journal*; Gillian Tett, Paul Davies, Henny Sender, and

Saskia Scholtes at the *Financial Times*; and Gretchen Morgenson and Jenny Anderson at the *New York Times*.

Financial bloggers also have become a major source. There are dozens and dozens of superb blogging sites—from market professionals, academics, and financial writers—that offer a wealth of data, insights, and gossip. Two that I check every day are FT Alphaville (ftalphaville.ft.com)—by *Financial Times* reporters—and Yves Smith's Naked Capitalism (www.nakedcapitalism.com).

Finally, my thanks to a number of friends who read all, or parts, of the manuscript and made many helpful comments, including Joan Hochman, Art Speigel, Herb Sturz, Dick Leone, and Andrew Kerr. And an extra thanks to my wife Beverly, who, besides her usual support and help, was a great jargon-antibody.

CHAPTER 1

The Death of Liberalism

For connoisseurs of misery, the ten years from 1973 through 1982 are a feast of low points.

The rate of economic growth was one of the worst for any comparable period since the end of World War II. The country endured one of the worst periods of inflation in American history, and foreign investors fled the dollar as if it were the Mexican peso.

Japanese companies humiliated American standard-bearers in one flagship industry after another. Layoffs and short shifts spread through heavy industry. America's once-humming industrial heartland transmuted into the Rust Belt.

The OPEC nations increased oil prices tenfold and strongarmed their way into ownership interests in Big Oil's production arms.

There were war protests and campus battles. Cities were awash in crime and disorder. New York City went to the edge of bankruptcy. A president was forced from office, and his vice president resigned over charges of bribery and corruption.

Helicopters evacuated Americans from the embassy rooftop in Saigon, fleeing a lost war. The Soviet Union visibly stepped up the missile race and sent 100,000 troops into Afghanistan. President Jimmy Carter spent the last months of his presidency negotiating ransom payments for fifty-two American hostages held by Iranian radicals.

Economists even came up with a measure of how awful it felt. In 1980, the Misery Index, the sum of the inflation rate and the unemployment rate, was the highest ever. An ugly new word, "stagflation," entered the political vocabulary.

Events so pervasive and so consequential are usually overly determined. There is no one cause, but *lots* of causes. The 1970s disasters had at least three primary roots—the loss of business vision, demographic shifts, and gross economic mismanagement.

Business Embraces Incompetence

Consider a listing of the top American companies from about 1910 or so: It would include U.S. Steel and Bethlehem Steel; Standard Oil and Gulf; Swift, Armour, and General Foods; AT&T, General Electric, and Westinghouse; Anaconda Copper and Alcoa; Dupont and American Tobacco. Then look at a listing from the late 1970s. Except for companies from new industries, like General Motors and RCA, it's much the same. Despite all the vicissitudes of mergers, name changes, and antitrust, the top companies in 1910 mostly held their positions for the next seventy years.

The winning companies of the early 1900s had emerged from the most savagely Darwinian industrial maelstrom in history. Rockefeller, Carnegie, and their ilk clawed to the top through ruthless efficiency and lethal execution. The best German or British chemical and steel companies could beat the Americans in this or that niche, but across the board, the United States possessed the most formidable array of industrial power ever seen.

And then Americans slacked off.

Almost as soon as U.S. Steel was born from a string of mergers in 1901, its chief, Elbert Gary, started working out market-sharing and price-maintenance agreements with his competition. U.S. Steel was born controlling more than half the market; Gary argued that if his fellow steel moguls just adopted U.S. Steel's high price structure, they would each maintain their market shares and all could flourish together. After the Standard breakup in 1911, the oil industry fell into a similar pattern, and eventually so did newer industries, like automobiles and televisions. A steel company chief once explained the logic of price maintenance to a Senate antitrust committee: "If we were to lower our prices, then it would be met by our competitors, and that would drop their profit, so we would still be right back to the same price relatively."

War preserved and extended Americans' lazy hegemonies. Companies could wax fat on wartime weapons orders and postwar reconstruction, and at the same time help destroy their overseas competitors. A 1950s steel sales executive bragged, "Our salesmen don't sell steel; they allocate it." But by defanging competition, Gary's system of "administered pricing" froze technology. The locus of innovation in steel-making shifted to Europe and Japan.

Big Labor was inducted into the system in the 1950s, with the General Motors formula for labor settlements. The industry price-setter usually took the lead in union negotiations. Contracts would normally cover three years and would include wage awards in line with forecasted productivity increases. Later, as inflation ticked up, contracts included both the expected productivity increase plus annual adjustments for inflation. But when productivity flattened out in the 1970s and inflation accelerated at the same time, the companies were left with a cost problem they could not wish away.

Even contemporaries understood that the 1950s and early 1960s were something of a golden age. Big-company pay-settlement standards percolated throughout the smaller companies that supplied them, and most companies were adding pension and health benefits. For a large slice of the population, the American dream of a house with a lawn and a decent school for the kids came true. John Kenneth Galbraith's *The Affluent Society* (1958) announced that the problem of production had been solved, that consumer wants were on the verge. of being sated, and that it was time to focus on "expelling pain, tension, sorrow, and the ubiquitous curse of ignorance."

Labor schools for union activists flourished in the 1950s and 1960s. Most of them were run by Catholics, many at Jesuit colleges. (The big industrial unions were often two-thirds Catholic.) The schools taught bargaining and organization techniques, labor law, and labor economics, while extolling the "solidarist" power-sharing arrangements characteristic of Catholic Europe. Businessmen often attended the courses.

Union leaders and executives began to regard themselves as industrial statesmen.

At the business schools, the reign of the big companies was taken as part of the natural order. The hot topics of the 1950s and 1960s were organization and finance, essentially rearranging furniture within the stable multi-unit enterprises of modern "managerial capitalism." There was a 1960s merger movement, but it had an academic, chalk-dust smell. The idea was that if companies assembled diverse portfolios of businesses, they could smooth out their earnings cycles. Absurdly, Exxon went into office equipment; Mobil bought a circus and a department store chain.

As business administration migrated to the graduate schools, executive ranks drifted farther from the shop floor. The consistent message of management textbooks from as late as the 1970s was that Ford, General Motors, and Dupont had written the sacred texts of production practices in the 1920s. The most important postwar developments were mathematical techniques for optimizing machine maintenance and inventories. You could work on the formulas without going near a factory.

Like flightless birds on a predator-free island, American companies had no defenses when hungry and hard-eyed competitors finally came hunting from overseas. It was a slaughter. By 1980, for all practical purposes, America no longer manufactured televisions or radios, the Germans and Japanese controlled the machine tool industry, and American steel and textile industries were a catastrophe. Even IBM's mainframe computers were being challenged powerfully by Amdahl and Fujitsu.

Spasmodic attempts to react to the foreign onslaught only revealed how incompetent American companies had become. During the years that Detroit was mesmerized by chrome-laden tailfins and theories of "planned obsolescence," companies like Toyota and Volkswagen introduced Americans to the advantages of small, well-made, fuel-efficient cars. Subcompact imports began to gain enough market share that Ford and Chevrolet responded with small cars of their own, the Pinto and the Vega, both introduced in 1970. When the oil price shocks hit in 1973 and small-car sales took off, the American entries were exposed as embarrassing duds—*Forbes* magazine later ranked them among the worst cars of all time.

The complacent incompetence of American business was bad enough. The demographic tides were a double whammy.

The Baby Boom

Ask an economist about the 1970s plunge in American productivity, and he will point to the falloff in investment. Sure, executives were slothful and incompetent, but rising inflation and interest rates made capital very expensive.

But a demographer would point to the upsurge in young workers. People in the baby boom generation entered their twenties in the 1970s, creating a huge influx of untrained, unskilled workers, reducing productivity, and creating downward pressure on wages. When workers are cheap and capital is expensive, it's sensible to reduce investment.

The baby boom illustrates the impact of marginal changes in a population cohort. Eighteen- to twenty-four-year-olds were 4.3 percent of the population in 1960, and 5.6 percent of the population in 1970, which looks like only modest change. But the total *numbers* of eighteen- to twenty-four-year-olds jumped by about 50 percent, from 7.6 million to 11.4 million, and that was utterly disruptive.

Richard Easterlin, who wrote one of the earliest and best analyses of the boomer phenomenon, emphasizes the size of a birth cohort compared to the one just before. Birth rates dropped sharply during the Depression years, so the generation of men entering the labor market in the 1950s was an unusually small one and was much in demand. The pay gap between young workers and older workers therefore became unusually narrow, facilitating early marriage and family formation. All measures of social disruption, like crime rates, dropped like a stone. Earlier marriage and greater economic security also made couples more willing to have children. In Easterlin's formulation, the cohort changes became self-amplifying.

Sometime in the mid-1950s, however, the amplifying mechanisms began tilting toward disruption. When the boomers reached school age, elementary schools everywhere were forced onto double and triple sessions; it was even worse in the suburbs, where schools had to be built from scratch. As they hit their teens, juvenile delinquency moved to the top of the social agenda. Struggling to cope, police forces became more selective about the behaviors that elicited an intervention, a process that Daniel Patrick Moynihan later called "defining deviance down."

The sixties brought a spike in college-age youngsters, multiplied by a sharp increase in the percentage of kids going to college. The heroic students who manned the front lines of the civil rights confrontations in the late 1950s and early

1960s set a pattern of student revolts against "oppressive" structures everywhere. When draft calls for the deepening war in Vietnam provoked violent campus protests, the ensuing confrontations between police and campus radicals took on a nasty class edge—the first skirmishes in the culture wars that would mark the country's politics for years to come.

Alarmed by spiraling crime and violence in central cities, President Lyndon Johnson pushed through his War on Poverty and Model Cities legislation, potpourris of 1920s-vintage social improvement schemes, wartime systems engineering, and modish concepts of self-empowerment. Urban welfare rolls jumped tenfold, riots flared through most major cities, and large swathes of poorer neighborhoods burned to the ground. Big companies fled downtowns, leaving mayors to grapple with plummeting tax rolls and escalating demands for security and services.

The sixties ended sometime in 1971. War protests were a major factor in Johnson's decision not to run for a second term in 1968. Richard Nixon claimed a secret plan for ending the war, but once in office he concentrated on "Vietnamization"—reducing U.S. casualties by shifting the brunt of the fighting to locals. Student protests flared over the incursions into Cambodia in 1970 but stopped abruptly when draft callups were ended the next year. Killings at a 1971 Florida rock concert exposed the violence and drugs at the underbelly of the counterculture.

Kevin Phillips's 1969 book, *The Emerging Republican Majority*, foresaw how disgust with the posturing of students and liberal elites, and weariness with rising crime and welfare spending, would push traditional Democratic working-class voters toward the Republican Party. Nixon's landslide win in the 1972 election, after narrowly edging out Hubert Humphrey in 1968, proved Phillips right.

When Nixon took office in 1969, the economy was already careening toward serious trouble, and he set about making the economic crisis about as bad as it could possibly be.

Mismanagement as Political Art

During the five years of Johnson's presidency, despite an uptick in inflation, the real, or inflation-adjusted, annual rate of growth exceeded 5 percent. But by 1970, Nixon's second year in office, growth plunged to near zero, while inflation was scraping 6 percent. Nixon was already planning his second presidential run, and those were dreadful numbers for a campaign launch.

But there was little room for maneuver. The 1970 federal deficit was as big as any Johnson had run. An attempt at fiscal stimulation was likely to spill over into more inflation. And then there was the dollar. The American commitment to redeem dollars at the rate of $35 per ounce of gold underpinned world monetary stability. But American gold reserves were dropping, so currency traders mounted dollar raids to test the Treasury's resolve. The textbook solution was to raise interest rates so foreigners would choose to hold their dollars. But with the economy so fragile, a rate increase could trigger a full-blown recession.

Few politicians had Nixon's gift for the bold stroke. In August 1971 he helicoptered his entire economics team to Camp David for a weekend that Herbert Stein, a member of the

Council of Economic Advisers, predicted "could be the most important meeting in the history of economics" since the New Deal. The following week, Nixon announced that he would cut taxes, impose wage and price controls throughout the economy, impose a tax surcharge on all imports, and rescind the commitment to redeem dollars in gold.

Politically, it was a masterstroke. With price controls in place, Nixon and his Federal Reserve chief, Arthur Burns, could gun up the money supply without worrying about price inflation—the money supply numbers jumped by more than 10 percent in 1971, at the time the biggest increase ever. Economic growth obediently revived and was back up over 5 percent by the 1972 election, or just what the political doctors ordered.

All in a single weekend, Nixon had delivered big business from union wage pressures, supplier price hikes, and foreign competition, while consumers were delighted with flat prices. The dollar ended 1971 at about $44 per ounce of gold. In gold terms, that is, America's trading partners took a 25 percent loss on their holdings. Japan was especially hard hit because they were sitting on very large dollar balances.

The extent of the economic damage became clear only after Nixon had engineered his landslide. The OPEC oil price hikes, which helped trigger the Great Inflation of the 1970s, were a direct consequence of floating the dollar. By 1973, when the OPEC nations tripled the price of oil, the dollar had fallen to about $100 per ounce of gold, or about a third of its previous value. In 1979, when OPEC tripled prices yet again, the dollar varied between $233 and $578 per ounce, so OPEC was still losing ground in gold terms. When the dollar plunged to $850 an ounce in 1980, the gold price of oil was as low as it had ever been. The real problem was that America had debased its currency.

The 1971 wage-and-price "ninety-day freeze," as it was originally billed, lasted for three years. Controls are always easier to put on than to take off. The underlying inflation builds to a point of explosiveness, while a thicket of rules offers profitable little crevices for the lucky or the well-connected. Congress finally forced an end to the controls, except for the price controls on domestic oil, in the spring of 1974, when Nixon was ensnared in the coils of Watergate. Removal of controls triggered double-digit inflation and the nasty recessions of 1974 and 1975. The decline of American competitiveness continued apace—in 1977, Chrysler averted bankruptcy only by dint of last-minute government loans.

Nixon's social conservatism, and the visceral hatred he inspired in traditional liberals, obscures the fact that, by contemporary definitions, he was among the most liberal of presidents. As the war wound down, he cut military spending sharply, pushed through the greatest expansion in Social Security benefits since the program's inception, and created the federal affirmative action programs that quickly spread through most major corporations and public institutions.

In economics, Nixon was a Keynesian through and through, with a taste for the directive style of top-down intervention typical of Europe. Supposedly conservative cabinet members held much the same views, including Treasury secretary and former corporate lawyer John Connelly and Housing secretary George Romney, the former chairman of American Motors. Romney pronounced at one point that

America's economy was "no longer based on the principle of free competitive enterprise." Even Burns, the epitome of crusty conservatism, justified the resort to wage and price controls, as he told Congress, because "the rules of economics are not working quite the way they used to."

Especially with respect to energy, the interventionalist bias was continued during Gerald Ford's post-Watergate interregnum and extended even further after Carter's election in 1976. When Carter announced his National Energy Plan, he called it the "Moral Equivalent of War." Columnist Russell Baker immediately dubbed it "MEOW," and it was doomed. Designed by too-brilliant-by-half Energy Secretary James Schlesinger, who had also served as Defense secretary under Nixon and Ford, it comprised a highly complex array of taxes, incentives, allocations, and pricing schemes, including different price schedules for "new" oil and "old," pre-1977, oil, a "windfall profits tax," special taxes on imports, a national "synfuels" corporation, and much, much more. Plans were also far advanced for introducing WW II–style gasoline ration books. Long lines, and occasionally real violence, became fixtures at the nation's filling stations.

In desperation, Carter attempted to create a voluntary version of the Nixon wage and price controls. As quarterly inflation hit almost 14 percent in the spring of 1979, the *New York Times* reported:

Carter administration economic officials expressed more despair than hope, saying that little could be done except to drive less, eat lower-cost pork, rather than beef, and not "speculate" in new houses. "I'm like a leaf floating in a macroeconomic ocean," Alfred E. Kahn, chairman of the Council on Wage and Price Stability, conceded at a news conference.

It's hard to exaggerate the foreign contempt for the Carter economic team. Here is a memorandum from the Federal Reserve's foreign exchange desk prepared for a 1979 Open Market Committee meeting:

> In the first two weeks following [our last] . . . meeting, the dollar came under repeated bouts of selling pressure, as the exchange market reacted negatively, first to the delay of President Carter's energy address, then to the address itself, then to the resignation of his cabinet, then to the list of those who were asked not to stay on.* . . . [It was] . . . seen not so much as an economic crisis as a crisis in leadership . . . [the inability] to shape a coherent economic policy and get it through Congress, and over what appears to be a continuing chaotic state of energy policy.

The last days of the Carter administration were dominated by the hostage crisis in Iran. The shah of Iran, a longtime American ally, was deposed by radical Islamicists in early 1979, greatly roiling oil markets. As the economy grew increasingly chaotic, Carter made his much-criticized "malaise" speech in July, in which he seemed to blame the American people for his troubles. In November, Iranians invaded the

---

* In July, apparently in an effort to demonstrate decisiveness, Carter asked his entire cabinet to resign, then reappointed most of them. The mandatory resignations extended down to the deputy assistant secretary levels and so involved hundreds of officials, suspending major policy-related activities for weeks.

American embassy in Tehran and took sixty-six Americans hostage. Fourteen were released over the next weeks and months, but the remaining fifty-two were held for 444 days. Carter retaliated by boycotting Iranian oil, which was risible, since suppliers freely trade oil with each other. Spotting weakness, the Soviets marched into Afghanistan six weeks later, so Carter canceled American wheat sales to the Soviets and boycotted the Moscow Olympics, infuriating American farmers and all Olympic fans. The next April, an attempted helicopter rescue operation, Desert One, was aborted without coming near its objective, and eight men were killed in an evacuation accident. Carter retreated to the White House Rose Garden and for the remainder of his administration concentrated on negotiating a release of the hostages.

Rarely had American prestige and pride sunk so low. Foreign policy was in shambles, and the economy was a mess. Inflation hit 13.5 percent in 1980, and output was dropping, while the dollar spiraled into the abyss. Carter deserves credit, however, for at least two accomplishments. Over the objections of Congress, he forced through an end to oil price controls, although the extended termination schedule meant that they were ended only during the Reagan presidency. And he appointed Paul Volcker head of the Federal Reserve and gave him a free hand in fighting inflation. It was the most important policy appointment of the era.

What Was Liberalism?

In its modern sense, liberalism is a theory of government posing as a branch of economics. Adam Smith and David Ricardo called their discipline political economy, a useful term. The "political" was dropped when the twentieth-century marriage of economics and advanced mathematics fostered the illusion that economics is a science. But the empirical underpinnings of public economics, the branches that seek to inform government policy, are often so fragile that they are better understood as ideologies.

The Keynesian version of political economy that John Kennedy ostentatiously brought to Washington in 1961 was an expression of faith in the potential of high intelligence employed in activist government. Built in part from nostalgic exaggerations of the accomplishments of the New Deal and the war administration, its central premise was that an economic intelligentsia could reliably employ government levers to achieve specific outcomes in the real world.

In practice, Kennedy's economic policies were cautious. The economic centerpiece of his short administration—generating a recovery with a tax cut—was implemented only well after a recovery was already under way. But the recovery still powerfully reinforced the mythology of central management, one that was later carried to the point of parody when Lyndon Johnson and his advisers gathered each night to choose the next day's bombing targets in Vietnam. For Richard Nixon the central attraction of Keynesian activism was how well it played with the public, as he had learned to his sorrow in the 1960 campaign. The main goal of Nixon's radical centralization of economic controls in 1971, after all, was a landslide reelection.

It is hard to exaggerate the faith of 1970s- and 1980s-vintage liberals in the power of a puppet-master government, especially in academia. (Academics are always suckers for arguments that extol the virtues of superior intelligence.) An early–1980s survey of America's industrial decline, co-edited by Laura Tyson, later chair of President Bill Clinton's Council of Economic Advisers, concluded that America's competitive woes came down to a lack of industrial policy. Competitiveness forums at the Massachusetts Institute of Technology detailed the government industrial policies required in a long series of specific industries. A study of Japan concluded:

> The only way America can counter the Japanese challenge and regain world leadership is through comprehensive use of an industrial policy. Without a strong central state and a top professional bureaucracy—the two preconditions of industrial policy—America is doomed to economic decline.

Superhuman powers were ascribed to the Japanese Ministry of Trade and Industry, the dreaded MITI, supposedly the nerve center of Japanese industrial conquest. Although MITI certainly pandered to the interests of the big Japanese cartels, its actual record in making strategic calls was quite mixed. In mainframe computers, the ministry imposed a relentless twenty-year drive to achieve parity with IBM—only to discover to its horror that it had picked the wrong target. By the time Japan's computer industry finally caught up to IBM in the late 1980s, the mainframe vendors were under siege from makers of distributed, microprocessor-based computing, in which Japan had almost no position.

But it was not just academics. Even Andrew Grove, chairman of Intel and one of the world's most brilliant and successful businessmen, fulminated darkly that America would become a "techno-colony" of Japan in the absence of a determined, MITI-like American riposte. The peak of the silliness may have been the push for government leadership in creating an American high-definition television set to compete with Sony's (which was based on obsolete nondigital technology).

Intellectuals are reliable lagging indicators, near-infallible guides to what used to be true. The infatuation with MITI-like strategies for America reached its peak just about the time Japan was entering an economic slough that was to drag on for fifteen painful years. The prolonged declines in both Germany and France over roughly the same period, if not as serious as Japan's, provoked widespread worries over incurable "eurosclerosis," caused by excessive government economic steering.

With the eclipse of Keynesian liberalism, the day had finally dawned for an alternative paradigm that had been waiting patiently in the wings—Milton Friedman's "monetarism."

Ostensibly, monetarism was a theory about money. Friedman's research in economic history convinced him that inflation was "always and everywhere a monetary phenomenon"—if the supply of money rises faster than real economic activity, prices will rise. Further, he was convinced that every economy had a natural rate of employment, defined by its technology and the skills of its workforce. Attempts at fiscal stimulation to increase employment beyond that rate were invariably inflationary.

Monetarists taught that the supply of money was the product of the *stock* of money—just the sum of spendable coins, bills, checking accounts, etc.—times its turnover rate, or its *velocity*. Friedman's historical research showed that velocity was roughly constant, so government policy need concern itself only with the money stock. If the Federal Reserve expanded the money stock at approximately the rate of economic growth, prices would also stay roughly constant. Most important, by establishing rigid rules for monetary management, it would constrain officials' meddlesome impulses.

Monetarism, in fact, proved extremely difficult to implement technically, but practical results have little to do with the persuasiveness of ideologies. While Keynesians prayed to the idol of the quasi-omniscient technocrat, the Friedmanite religion enshrined the untrammeled workings of free-market capitalism. (Friedman opposed almost all forms of government regulation, including safety regulation for pharmaceuticals.)

Ronald Reagan's election in 1980 signaled that Keynesian liberalism was dead. Vaguely, inchoately, but unquestionably, voters had signaled their readiness for a change of ideological horses. The theorists of the free market would get to run their race.

CHAPTER 2

Wall Street Finds Religion

Frank Knight, one of the founders of the Chicago school of free-market capitalism, most famously represented by Milton Friedman, once prefaced an economics textbook with the statement: "It is somewhat unusual to begin the treatment of a subject with a warning against attaching too much importance to it; but in the case of economics, such an injunction is quite as much needed as explanation and emphasis of the importance it really has."

Knight's caution was prescient, for in its modern form, Chicago school economics has mutated from a style of analysis into a Theory of Everything. For almost any public or social issue, adherents believe, the free market, if allowed to work without obstruction, will consistently produce optimum outcomes. The omnivorous streak in Chicago economics has drawn it into the realms of crime, welfare, education, health care, and other areas once thought to be mostly outside economics' purview.

Multitudes of conservatives were converted to the ranks of free-market dogmatists by two dramatic events at the outset of the 1980s. The first was the surge of venture capital investment after a sharp 1978 cut in the capital gains tax. The second was the collapse of the OPEC cartel after President Reagan pushed through the final decontrol of oil prices in early 1981. Neither episode, in fact, was quite what it seemed.

An obscure Republican Congressman named William Steiger pushed through a cut in the capital gains tax in April 1978, a moment that Robert Bartley, then editor of the *Wall Street Journal*, spotlighted as "the morning it all started to come true . . . [when] a decade of envy came to its close, and the search for a growth formula started in earnest." It was "Steiger," according to Bartley, that unleashed the boom in venture investment that supercharged the growth of companies like Apple, Compaq, and Sun Microsystems in computers, Genentech in biotech, and even old-business revolutionaries like FedEx.

The prosaic truth is that the surge in venture investing had its roots in a 1973 law requiring companies to set aside money to fund their pension promises to workers. Pension fund assets quickly ballooned to $1 trillion, and pension fund managers clamored for more leeway in the strict pension fund investing rules. When the regulations were finally eased in 1979, it was pension funds, foundations, and endowments that were the source of most of the new venture money. Those investors are tax-exempt, of course, and couldn't have cared less about "Steiger." It's not that tax rates don't matter. It's just that if you try to trace exactly *how much* they matter, the usual answer is "not a lot."*

Steiger's tax cut has the status of a foundation myth among the free-market faithful but is otherwise not widely known. The price-decontrol/OPEC-collapse story, however, was obvious to anyone who drove a car.

One of Reagan's first official acts upon assuming the presidency in 1981 was to eliminate the last vestiges of oil price controls. Just a few months later, the *Times* pointed out in some wonder that "All over the country, gas stations . . . have been shaving prices. . . . The outlook for the summer driving season . . . hasn't been so bright in years." By the fall, energy prices were in free fall. According to a still-amazed *Times*, "A number of experts contend controls had the perverse effect of actually increasing consumer prices, rather than holding them down"—which Chicago economists had been shouting for years.

The scale and speed of the apparent price response was astonishing. Consumers cut down on optional driving and shifted to more fuel-efficient cars. Houses and household appliances, office buildings, and manufacturing plants were redesigned or retooled for greater energy efficiency. Oil production soared in marginal fields once thought beyond re-

---

* The burst of startup activity was also driven by demographics. I belonged to the senior management group of a large bank in the early 1980s. Almost all of us were in our early forties. We supervised hundreds and hundreds of ambitious thirtysomething baby boomers facing promotion channels that were hopelessly clogged. The big companies that were our customers all had the same problem, and most of them were downsizing, to boot. Of course there was a surge of start-ups.

covery. By 1988, crude oil prices, in inflation-adjusted terms, were lower than they were in 1973. After a decade of swaggering spending, OPEC members were desperate for foreign exchange and continually broke cartel production agreements. To the ill-concealed pleasure of Western pundits, camels made a comeback as desert transport, picking their way among rusting Mercedes limousines.

But as with "Steiger," the real story is much duller. The ratio of national output to energy inputs, it turns out, started improving sharply in 1973, by about 2 percent a year, with no help from the Chicago school. (Before 1973, the energy/GDP ratio was worsening.) The improvement was even faster during the Reagan years, by about 2.6 percent a year, but that's hardly a discontinuity. Moreover, an analysis by the U.S. Department of Energy suggests that much of the 1980s gains came from forced downsizing in energy-intensive sectors, like steel, and the shift to services, rather than from efficiency improvements. OECD data show roughly similar energy efficiency gains throughout the world over the same time span.

So why did the price break happen in 1981? In all likelihood, seven years of global efficiency gains, coupled with the 1981 recession, which was substantially global in its effect, unbalanced OPEC's demand/supply assumptions. That happened to coincide with the peak of the Iran-Iraq war, when Arabs were pouring money into Iraq to forestall an Iranian victory. War spending and the profligacy of OPEC members made it difficult for them to accommodate a production cutback. Member indiscipline fractured the cartel, and prices collapsed to the point that eliminated cartel returns.

In other words, the market worked. But it worked over the long haul, across multiple regimes and policy dispensations, reflecting tidal currents, like the advanced-country shift toward services, that policy-makers were only dimly aware of. Decontrolling oil prices in January 1981 was a sensible policy move, but it did not break OPEC. A second important, if modest, lesson is that the Carter administration could have achieved much the same efficiency gains without the Sturm und Drang of the rationing attempts. The entire story, in short, is consistent with Knight's dictum about the value of economics, and the importance of not exaggerating it.

Killing Inflation

When Carter appointed Paul Volcker Federal Reserve chairman in 1979, it was probably the darkest period of his presidency, with both Wall Street and foreign finance ministries sounding emergency alarms. Volcker was at best a third choice. President of the New York Fed, the most important of the district Federal Reserve banks, he was a financial economist who had divided his career between the Treasury and the Chase Manhattan Bank. He was known to be conservative, extremely knowledgeable in the intricacies of financial markets, a hawk on inflation, and a strong leader. To Carter insiders, he was "the candidate of Wall Street."

Volcker was taking on one of the two or three most important jobs in the world—to cut inflation and restore financial order, in whatever way he thought fit. Inflation had traumatized long-term investors, siphoning money away from the bonds and stocks that financed businesses and fueling hard asset bubbles in gold, art, and real estate. On spot markets, the dollar price of oil was going up 6 percent a month; gold had jumped 28 percent in a single month. A Weimar-type hyperinflation wasn't inconceivable.

People were scared—union members and business leaders alike. It was not just the steep recession, but a recession accompanied by runaway inflation, which had never before happened in the United States. Recessions come and go. But inflation just kept steadily marching upward, in good times and bad, flashing a red signal that the economy was out of control.

Volcker took over as chairman when Milton Friedman's monetarism was gaining a strong following in Washington. For Friedman, monetarism was in part a device to limit the purposeful meddling of central government. He taught that inflation could be controlled solely by controlling the stock of money—the quantity of M1, the sum of all check money and all circulating cash. If the Fed merely ensured that the stock of money grew at roughly the same pace as the economy, all prices would remain on an even keel.

Volcker was never a committed monetarist, but after several months on the job, amid much concern in Europe and in the financial press, he decided to make a dramatic demonstration of his determination to end inflation by formally adopting a monetarist strategy. There is "certainly some truth in the monetarist position," he told me almost thirty years later, "and I found it useful, both as a way to explain what we were doing, and as a way to discipline ourselves." At the same time, when he discussed his strategy with members of the Federal Open Market Committee (FOMC), he warned them that money numbers were very slippery and they might easily find themselves grossly missing their targets "after making a hulla-baloo about this change in technique."

The shift in policy was announced at an unusual evening press conference, and he got the desired shock effect. Amid a sharp sell-off on Wall Street, the *New York Times* editorialized under the headline "Mr. Volcker's Verdun": "Mr. Volcker is a gambler. He is betting high, with a poor hand. The entire nation needs to hope that he beats the odds."

The truth is that monetarism didn't break inflation, Volcker did. Somehow, free-market monetarists hadn't guessed that if the Fed cracked down on conventional money stock, profit-seeking banks would create new financial techniques to avoid the restrictions. Which they promptly did—spinning out high-yielding money market mutual funds, interest-bearing checking accounts, electronic sweeps to marshal corporate cash, and much more. The transcripts of FOMC meetings through most of 1980 betray an air of semicomic desperation as the members try to discern which numbers they should count as the money supply.

Volcker broke inflation simply by clamping down very hard and very persistently, using every weapon at his disposal—interest rates, money supply, jawboning. By January 1981, Fed Funds, the basic short-term interest rate, were at an unheard-of 19 percent, while three-month Treasury bills were paying 20 percent. The economy slipped into recession in the second quarter, and as the Fed's grim tightening continued in the teeth of a deeper and deeper downslide, howls of protest rose in the Congress. To his credit, Reagan made a ringing state-ment of support in April: "[N]either this administration nor the Federal Reserve will allow a return to the fiscal and monetary policies of the past that have created the current conditions." In 1982, the growth in GDP was a negative 1.9 percent, the worst in the postwar era.

To an amazing degree, people put up with it. One of the district Fed presidents reported at a spring 1982 FOMC meeting that both business executives and labor leaders in his region were resolved to see it through. "[E]ven from the labor group," he said, "there was a strong recognition, and hope really, that we will continue to look to solving the long-term fundamental problem rather than reacting to the pain of the moment." That same spring, Volcker accepted an invitation to speak to the home builders' convention—with some trepidation, since they were among the hardest-hit of all industry sectors. Volcker's message was uncompromising: "[If] we let up on our anti-inflation effort . . . the pain we have suffered would have been for naught—and we would only be putting off to some later time an even more painful day of reckoning." To his surprise, he got a standing ovation.

Inflation—blessedly—broke in mid-1982, and the consumer price index (CPI) was essentially flat during the second half of the year. By year-end, Fed Funds were down to a reasonable 8.7 percent. Growth was barely positive in the fourth quarter but turned in a respectable 4.5 percent in 1983 and a booming 7.2 percent in 1984. The dollar soared. Much to the dismay of Republicans, who were trying to win a presidential election, Volcker cracked down yet again in mid-1984 and once again got unequivocal public support from Reagan. Real GDP was still very strong for the full year, before settling down to a respectable 4.1 percent in 1985, while the inflation rate dropped to a spectacular 1.9 percent, a twenty-year low.

Wall Street was finally convinced: The interest rate on long-term Treasury bonds dropped and, with only mild interruptions, continued to fall for the next twenty years. The grim demonstration of what America would endure to protect its currency transformed the world's impression of its economic management. From that point, America's commitment to price stability was assumed as a matter of course.

Two Market Parables

Unusually for a president, Reagan was a man of simple and consistent principles. The clarity and determination of his anti-Sovietism was arguably a major factor in the demise of the regime. In economics, he believed strongly in the core principles of the Chicago school—lower taxes, free markets, minimal regulation. In practice, the record was mixed. Two of the major economic stories of the 1980s—the leveraged buyout, or LBO, boom and the savings and loan crisis—demonstrate both the power and limitations of markets.

The LBO boom lasted from about 1982 to 1989. For roughly the first four years, it was an object lesson in the transformational power of free markets. The underperforming, top-heavy conglomerates that had failed so miserably against foreign competition were stripped down, torn apart, and refocused—clearing out nonproductive layers of management and hiving off noncore assets, like Goodyear's hotel businesses or steel companies' railroads.

Buyout managers turned textile companies into high-productivity specialists—Fieldcrest and Cannon in towels and sheets, Stevens and Collins & Aikman in auto body cloth. Gordon Cain rolled up a number of small chemical companies to assemble one of the most productive specialty chemical businesses in the world. Lexmark, created from a buyout of IBM's personal printer business, became a market force as soon as it was freed from the bureaucracy. There were hundreds of deals like these, most of them "friendly," and often engineered by second- and third-tier executives frustrated by change-resistant top managers.

Comatose stock markets jittered back into life, and by about 1986, average P/E multiples (stock price divided by per-share earnings) had tripled. By all historical standards, stocks were aggressively priced. That was the cue for the market gods to appear on a mountaintop and announce the end of slam-dunk deals. The rational investor would slow down and start sifting for value.

Instead, the markets went crazy. Returns on the first wave of deals were so spectacular that big investors, like pension funds and endowments, were clamoring to get in, while fund start-ups multiplied like roaches. Unlike, say, steelmaking, financial markets offer opportunities for very large, very fast returns, drawing in sharp operators usually with money lent to them by banks.

With more and more money chasing deals, structures got much more complicated, with bond piled on bond. A favorite was "payment in kind," or PIK, bonds—if you missed a payment, the creditor was given more bonds. Wall Streeters joked about the "death spiral"—repeated missed payments triggered more and more PIK issuances until the debt load spun into infinity. PIKs have recently reappeared in the more aggressive 2007 private equity takeovers.

The Decade of Greed, as the deal frenzy came to be called, lasted from about 1986 to 1989. Once the hysteria broke, the collapse took only months. A spectacular bidding war for United Airlines in the summer of 1989 ended, shockingly, when the banks refused financing. Long-awaited deals in the pipeline were quickly scuttled. Then in January, Federated Department Stores, only thirteen months after its buyout, announced it could not pay debt service. A string of similar announcements followed in short order. Revco (drugstores), it turned out, was insolvent on the day the deal closed, although the bankers and fund managers had extracted $80 million in fees. Remember, the people buying those bonds were *sophisticated* investors.

The second case, the crisis in the savings and loan, or S&L, industry, was almost pure economic waste and is a signal demonstration of the importance of regulatory oversight of lending institutions in modern financial markets.

S&Ls gathered local deposits and financed local residential mortgages, almost always at fixed rates. When the 1970s inflation and money market funds pushed competitive deposit rates up to 20 percent, S&Ls were effectively out of business.

A bipartisan rescue bill somewhat pointlessly prolonged the agony. Much more damaging was the appointment of an antiregulatory doctrinaire, Richard Pratt, as chief S&L regulator, for he proceeded to gut virtually all regulatory prohibitions against self-dealing.

By the time Pratt had finished, it was possible for a single individual to take control of an S&L, then organize and lend to multiple subsidiaries—for land acquisition, construction, building management, and the like—and create his own small real estate empire entirely with depositors' money. Or more commonly, to *pretend* to create a real estate empire while siphoning deposits into, say, personal jet planes, a favorite in Texas.

From 1980 through 1984, an operator named Charles Knapp ballooned a California S&L's loans on the books from $1.7 billion to $40 billion before the government finally forced him out. His good loans were eventually sold for about $500 million. Another owner with a $1.8 billion loan book had bought six Learjets before the Feds noticed that 96 percent of his loans were delinquent. As late as 1988, 132 *insolvent* Texas S&Ls were still growing rapidly.

Sadly, some of the proudest names on Wall Street got in on the scam; the records of law firms and accounting firms were especially depressing. Among the venerable law firms paying multimillion-dollar settlements were Jones, Day, Reavis, and Pogue; Paul, Weiss, Rifkind; and Kaye Scholer. The total tab to the accounting profession for legal fees, fines, and settlements was estimated at $800 million. Ernst & Young and Arthur Andersen (later of Enron fame) paid especially big settlements. The total taxpayer cost, of course, was many times the settlement recoveries.

What morals can be drawn from those tales? For one thing, free markets do work, just as they did in resolving the oil crisis. Japan and Europe both were clearly outperforming America at the outset of the decade, and both were flagging badly by the end. And since both intentionally buffer market processes in the interest of stability, it took them a very long time to work their way out of their late-1980s doldrums—in Japan's case, the better part of two decades. In the United States, by contrast, the forced-pace 1980s corporate housecleaning, roughshod as it was, cleared the ground for the lean, high-productivity economy that America became in the 1990s.

But the second half of the LBO boom and the S&L debacle demonstrate the dangers of loose financial markets regulation. In raw markets, the scent of money deadens all other sensory and ethical organs. In both cases the quick, the deadly, and the unprincipled made a lot of money fast, while ordinary workers and the taxpayer took it in the ear.

Interlude: The Goldilocks Economy of the 1990s

Virtually the entire economic profession was forecasting a serious global recession when Bill Clinton assumed the presidency. He came with a detailed economic stimulus plan that had been a central platform of his campaign. Instead he got caught in a bizarre Democratic conversion experience—a sudden dawning that *budget deficits* were the root of all economic evil and that expunging them was the surest road to recovery. The deficit hawks, led by Robert Rubin, then head of the Domestic Policy Council and late of Goldman Sachs, held that deficits absorbed savings, raised interest rates, and slowed investment and growth. If you convinced the bond market that you were serious about lowering deficits, they would respond by lowering interest rates, and all good things would follow.

Rubin carried the day, although Clinton almost failed to carry his party. The final budget bill, almost pure tax increase, was rammed through only by an all-out, down-to-the-wire drive, and finally was passed on a tiebreaking Senate vote by Vice President Al Gore.

And just as the Rubinites had promised, Clinton miraculously got his boom—aka the dot-com bubble.

Few people had even heard of the World Wide Web and the Internet before a start-up company called Netscape—it sold the first Web browser ordinary people could use—executed its public stock issuance in August 1995. The stock tripled on the first day, and within a few months, Jim Clark, a Silicon Valley veteran who was Netscape's primary investor, was the world's first dot-com billionaire. The tech stock boom was on.

As the frenzy fed on itself, Federal Reserve chairman Alan Greenspan worried publicly about "irrational exuberance" in 1996, then reversed himself a year later, cautiously accepting the possibility of a "new paradigm"—presaging an era of technology-enabled noninflationary growth. It was a remark almost guaranteed to increase the giddiness.

Bubbles are almost always anchored in real developments. The Web and the Internet were a true revolution, probably as important as the railroads. Secure, Web-enabled communication flattened out organizational charts in big companies, blew away layers of bureaucracy, tied together customers and suppliers, and allowed seamless outsourcing of noncore tasks. Productivity growth in the last half of the decade ran at an extremely high annual rate of 4 percent-plus.

Greenspan, himself something of an antiregulatory zealot, has never believed that asset bubbles are the business of the Fed. During the most riotous years of the LBO boom, he chose not to curtail bank lending for highly leveraged transactions until far too late, and in the late 1990s, he refused to tighten stock margin rules to take some air out of the tech bubble.

The implosion of the tech bubble came only after Clinton had already turned over the White House keys, allowing him to leave office with a gaudy set of economic accomplishments. Over his entire administration, real growth had averaged 3.7 percent, the best postwar record except for the Kennedy/Johnson years. The inflation record, at an average of 2.8 percent, was the best since Eisenhower's. Long bond rates hovered in the mid–5 percent range through most of 1998 and 1999, the lowest levels since the 1960s. And during Clinton's last three years in office, the government ran surpluses in excess of $300 billion, the best performance in the postwar era.

How did he do it? The official line, pushed especially hard by Rubin, is that it was through the application of "Rubinomics"—cutting deficits to lower interest rates. It is the same order of nonsense as the supply-sider's insistence that all booms are rooted in tax cuts. Rafts of studies by both liberal and conservative economists show that big deficit reductions move long-term interest rates by a few tenths of a percent, if at all. The deficit-cutting effect of Clinton's tax increase, in any case, was overwhelmed by the upsurge in gains taxes from the riotous stock market.

The 1990s boom, in fact, was rooted in the confluence of a host of much broader forces that almost ensured solid growth. The baby boomers, the generation that had so decisively stamped its imprint on every decade since the 1950s, were entering their forties and fifties—the years of greatest work output and savings. There was a productivity boom in American factories. The boomer generation of managers not only absorbed Japanese practices but also drew on uniquely American developments in distributed computing and digital communications that were just coming into full flower. After a decade of overinvestment in real estate, the vast flow of liquidity in pension and mutual funds was shifting back to stocks and bonds. The senior population was flat, military spending was falling, and new surpluses from a 1983 Social Security tax increase were cutting into the big Reagan-era deficits. Put all that together, and falling interest rates and strongly rising financial markets looked inevitable.

Then there were the forty years of government investment that designed and implemented the Internet, including most of its core technologies, built it into a working worldwide system, and developed the strategy and organizational model for shifting the Internet from government to private-sector control in 1995. Compared to such tidal developments, the Rubin tax increase was background static.

Despite its unevenness, the 1980s and 1990s economic experience strengthened conservative conviction in two core principles. The first, which had been amply demonstrated by the recoveries of the early 1980s and the 1990s, was the great power of free markets. The second was the importance of nearly fully deregulated financial markets, which was odd, since multiple market bubbles were a strong argument to the contrary.

In the next chapter, we'll explore some specific instruments and trading tools that were brought to a high level of development in the 1980s and 1990s and became the essential technologies in creating the credit bubble of the 2000s.

CHAPTER 3

Bubble Land:
Practice Runs

Although exciting new technologies fueled the dot-com boom, the bubble itself was a standard case of stock market hype and overshoot. But the decade from the late 1980s to the late 1990s also saw three other, much different boom-and-bust cycles. There was a big crash in residential mortgages in 1994 and two big trading-based crises—the 1987 stock market crash and the 1998 Long-Term Capital Management crisis, which the Federal Reserve at one point feared might bring down the whole global finance system.

All three of those episodes arose from fundamentally new investment technologies, enabled by breakthroughs in desktop computing and by an influx of mathematics PhDs to Wall Street. The new "quants" could carve up and reassemble old-fashioned asset classes so they were custom-fit to investor needs. Large-volume computerized trading could exploit tiny changes in stock prices or interest rates. Very broad new classes of complex, structured investment instruments revolutionized wholesale banking. All the new technologies and strategies harbored dangerous flaws that tended to reveal themselves only at points of great stress. Bigger, better, even more far-reaching versions of these strategies have now, in 2008, placed the entire global economy at risk.

The Rise, Fall, and Recovery of Mortgage-Backeds

The New Deal adopted S&Ls, or savings-and-loan banks, as the linchpin of its strategy for broadening opportunities for home ownership. To keep S&Ls in lendable funds, the government also created quasi-federal agencies—Fannie Mae, Ginnie Mae, and Freddie Mac*—that could liquefy local lending markets by buying up mortgages from S&Ls and other qualified lenders. The agencies in turn learned to maintain their own liquidity by selling mortgage-backed securities, or mortgage passthroughs. A pass-through is created by transferring a slug of mortgages to a trust, which in turn issues certificates representing a pro rata slice of all the principal and interest it receives. A

---

* Fannie Mae, the Federal National Mortgage Association (FNMA), was created in 1938 as a government agency to guarantee qualified mortgages and to issue bonds to finance the purchase of mortgages from qualified lenders. It was privatized in 1968 and is now owned by private shareholders. Ginnie Mae, the Government National Mortgage Association (GNMA), was spun out of the Fannie privatization to back certain classes of mortgages; unlike those of Fannie and Freddie, its bonds are federally guaranteed. Freddie Mac, the Federal Home Loan Mortgage Corporation (FHLMC), was created in 1970 as a Fannie clone to provide competition to Fannie. The definitions of eligible mortgages have steadily expanded over time.

trust comprising $100 million in mortgages paying an average interest rate of 6 percent would sell a certificate entitling the investor to, say, 1 percent of the trust proceeds. The investor would therefore collect 1 percent of $6 million each year, adjusted for her share of defaults or principal repayment proceeds, until all the mortgages were paid down.

Big investors were never completely delighted with mortgage pass-throughs. One problem is the "barbelled" nature of many institutions' investment appetites—they tend to invest on either extreme of the risk spectrum, putting most of their assets into supersafe instruments and a smaller allocation into high-yield/high-risk paper. Mortgages fell somewhere in the middle—not quite safe enough for the triple-A buyers, but without the returns to stir the pulses of yield-chasers. The monthly payment streams from mortgages were awkward (most bonds pay twice a year) and home mortgages have uncertain maturities. Whenever interest rates fall, homeowners rush to refinance, and if rates are rising, they hold on to their mortgages forever. Unexpected shifts in maturities can devastate investor returns.

Most of those problems were solved by the collateralized mortgage obligation (CMO), invented in 1983 by Larry Fink and a First Boston team on behalf of Freddie Mac. Mortgages were transferred to a trust, just as in a pass-through, but the mortgages were then sliced, or tranched, horizontally into three segments, with different bonds for each segment. The trick was that the top-tier bonds, which represented, say, 70 percent of the value sold, had first claim on *all* cash flows. Since it's inconceivable that 30 percent of a normal mortgage portfolio can default, top-tier bonds got triple-A, supersafe ratings and paid commensurately low yields. The second tranche typically included the next 20 percent of mortgages and sold at a somewhat higher yield, while the third tranche, covering the last 10 percent, was the first to absorb all losses. But since it also absorbed all the yield savings from the top-rated bonds, it could pay very attractive junk-bond-type yields. CMOs, in short, looked and paid just like bonds and offered yield choices to satisfy appetites across the entire risk spectrum.

The CMO was a genuinely important invention and had a profound impact on the mortgage industry. Traditionally, mortgage lenders were one-stop shops—they interviewed applicants, approved the credits, held the mortgages, collected the monthly payments, and managed default workouts and foreclosures. Within a few years of the advent of the CMO, however, the industry decomposed into highly focused sub-sectors. Mortgage brokers solicited and screened applicants. Thinly capitalized mortgage banks bid for the loans and held them until they had enough to support a CMO. Investment banks designed and marketed the CMO bonds. Servicing specialists managed collections and defaults. Fierce competition led to razor-thin margins at every step. And since CMOs were so much more attractive to investors, the interest premium, or spread, over Treasuries steadily dropped. An academic study concluded that by the mid-1990s, CMOs saved homeowners $17 billion a year. It is a classic illustration of the social contribution of financial innovation.

But the line between market success and market mania is a thin one. The first CMOs were so profitable that all the Wall Street firms jumped in, scarfing up mortgages and pumping them out as CMOs. The competitive scramble led to more and more complicated structures. (Creating floating-rate CMOs from pools of fixed-rate mortgages wasn't easy, but if investors wanted it, ingenious tranching could do it.)* The CMO desk at Kidder Peabody, headed by a youthful math whiz named Michael Vranos, was the most aggressive, dominating the CMO market almost as Michael Milken's Drexel Burnham had done in junk bonds.

The complexity of the instruments spiraled into absurdity. In 1983, modeling the payout scenarios on Fink's comparatively simple three-tranche CMO took a mainframe computer a whole weekend. But by the 1990s, when Sun workstations were standard furniture, CMO shops gleefully spewed out phantasmagorical 125-tranche instruments that no one could possibly understand. No matter how clever the structuring, however, a CMO was still a closed system: All the tranches drew their payouts from the same pool of mortgages. The more you tweaked a higher-rated tranche, the more violent the impact on the low-rated slivers at the bottom of the pile, or the "toxic waste," as it was known.

Disposing of the toxic waste soon became the primary limit on growth. Firms could carry some on their own balance sheets, and more could be fobbed off on innocents like newly wealthy Indian tribes and doctors' retirement funds, but those

---

*You created two tranches—one floated with a reference interest rate, usually LIBOR (the lending rate big banks charge each other in London), while the second one floated in the opposite direction. If LIBOR went up, it went down, which could be useful for hedging. Because it was harder to sell the inverse floaters, the inverse tranche might be only half as big as the floating tranche but would move twice as much.

were small markets. The secret of Kidder's growth is that it had been purchased by a deep-pocketed partner, GE, with an almost unlimited balance sheet and not a clue about what Kidder was up to. For an adventurous trader, dumb money is like a fairy godmother.

The party ended in the spring of 1994 when, in a surprise move, the Federal Reserve raised the funds rate by 1/2 percent, throwing all CMO math into confusion. David Askin, one of the most sophisticated of the CMO quants, became the poster boy for the subsequent crash. He ran a hedge fund with a $2 billion CMO position, primarily in the toxic waste, with a leverage ratio (total positions to equity) of about 3:1. When the Fed's rate rise automatically reduced the value of fixed-income assets, Askin's lenders had the right to demand additional cash or securities to secure their loans. The question was: What were Askin's securities worth? These were exotic instruments that were almost never traded, so the prices were set by models, but Askin's and the banks' models produced different results. Askin was eventually forced to sell some of his paper, and he discovered that there were no buyers—in effect, the market price plunged toward zero. Bear Stearns, the most aggressive of the bankers, moved to seize Askin's assets. Fearful of being shut out, the other banks came barreling in behind Bear. In hardly more than the blink of an eye, Askin and his investors had lost everything. The entire CMO market came to a screeching halt.

Kidder lasted only a couple months longer. GE's CEO, Jack Welch, discovered that his cherished new investment bank, the one that had just been featured on the cover of *Institutional Investor* as the cleverest around, was hemorrhaging money. That was not the GE way. Kidder Peabody was perhaps the most venerable firm on the Street; founded in 1864, it was one of the pioneers of American investment banking. But it was summarily shut down, its valuable assets sold off to Paine Webber, while Fink was brought in to work off Vranos's positions. Vranos, of course, survived and became a mega-rich mortgage-backed hedge fund manager. As of the fall of 2007, he may be caught in a déjà vu experience, for he has been forced to suspend investor redemptions from his funds.

Total losses in the CMO crash were about $55 billion, or about 5 percent of a trillion-dollar market, but the disruption was such that it took two or three years for mortgage markets to recover.

On the surface, the two quant-trading crises—the 1987 stock market crash and the Long-Term Capital Management disaster—appear quite different from CMOs, but as we'll see, there are consistent themes.

The 1987 Stock Market Crash

The Dow Jones Average broke 1,000 for the first time in 1968 and then stayed stuck in the 800–900 range for fifteen long, gloomy years, even as its value was eaten away by inflation. If you held on to the Dow stocks over that period, in inflation-adjusted terms you lost two-thirds of your money.

The early leveraged buyout deals created some stirrings in the stock indexes, but the market didn't really wake up until inflation turned in 1983. A bull market was soon in full roar; by the summer of 1987, the Dow had tripled. In June, the price/earnings (P/E) multiple on the S&P 500 stock index topped 21—in pre-dot-com days, that was very frothy, the fifth-highest in postwar history. Professionals knew the market was high but thought they had protected themselves with a new quant product, dubbed portfolio insurance, that was supposed to minimize losses in a market downturn.

Portfolio insurance was one of a basket of trading and hedging technologies Wall Street was introducing to better serve megacustomers, like pension and mutual funds. The common threads were the use of derivatives, advanced portfolio math, and heavy reliance on computers.

Derivatives, like options and futures, derive their value from other instruments. An option is the right, but not the obligation, to buy or sell a stock at a specific price within a specific time. In September 2007, IBM was trading at about 113. For about $7, you could buy a call option, or the right to buy IBM at 115 by January 2008. If you bought the calls, and the stock rose to 130, you could exercise the option—i.e., buy the stock at 115—and make $15 on a $7 investment. If you think shares will fall, on the other hand, you can buy a put, which gives you the right to sell at a specific price.

Financial futures, on the other hand, are firm contracts to buy or sell a security at a specific future date. A great attraction of financial futures is that cash margins are settled up daily. Suppose you sell a thirty-day future on Treasuries with a face value of $100,000 and delivery price at 95 (or $95,000) and that they're currently trading at 95. If they fall to 92, your counterparty has to post $3,000 in margin; if they rise to 96, she gets her margin back, and you have to post $1,000, and so on. At the end of the contract period, the margin debits and credits will exactly match the gains and losses from an actual trade of the instruments.

Options and futures markets exploded with the advent of the Black-Scholes formula, the most famous equation in the history of finance. If you plug currently known variables (the risk-free interest rate, the term of the option, the price and volatility of the stock, and the strike price of the option) into the Black-Scholes formula, it solves for the price of the option. Since any financial transaction can be cast in the form of an option, Black-Scholes became a tool for pricing everything. With a universal pricing tool, moreover, quant-oriented portfolio managers can convert almost any asset into almost any other—a portfolio of cash and options or futures, for example, can be made to behave just like a stock portfolio; floating-rate bonds can mimic fixed-rate bonds, and so on. Synthetic trading strategies executed with options and futures are often more efficient and less expensive than trading the underlying instruments, and often easier to mask from the competition, so they became an essential tool of megaportfolio asset management.

The portfolio insurance that so enamored big investors was actually a futures-based hedging strategy. An inexpensive way to hedge, or to protect a broad stock portfolio from a market fall, is to sell stock index futures. (Futures on indexes like the S&P 100 are traded on the Merc—the Chicago Mercantile Exchange.) If stocks rise, you'll lose money on the futures, but if stocks fall, your futures profits will offset your market loss. The specifics were devised by two University of California–Berkeley finance professors,

Hayne Leland and Mark Rubinstein. The investor chooses a desired price floor for the portfolio, then Black-Scholes-type math is used to design the futures strategy. When a portfolio is well above its floor, future sales are minimal, but if a portfolio starts to fall, future sales steadily increase to keep gains and losses roughly balanced. Leland and Rubinstein started a company to execute the hedging strategy for big investors, and within months most of the Wall Street firms were selling similar services. By the fall of 1987, some $100 billion of stock portfolios were "insured." Implementing the strategy required delegating the calculations and trading to computers.

After the Dow hit a new high of 2,700 in August 1987, the market began a slow, nervous slide through the fall, opening at just above 2,500 on Wednesday, October 14th. It was a week of jitter-making news—a brief shooting spat with Iran, a surprisingly big trade deficit, open disagreement between America and Europe on the management of the dollar, rising bond yields, a proposal to tax corporate takeovers. The Dow dropped 4 percent on Wednesday, and the overnight returns from Tokyo and London were even worse.

On Thursday morning, the portfolio insurance programs, which mostly operated on a one-day lag, kicked in with a vengeance. Prices on the futures and stock markets normally move in tight lockstep—otherwise, arbitrageurs swoop in to buy the cheap instrument and sell the other. But the sudden wave of insurance-related selling overwhelmed the Merc, severing the link between futures and stock prices. Chaotic conditions prevailed most of Thursday and much of Friday, with stocks often trailing well behind plummeting futures. From

Wednesday through Friday, the markets fell by more than 10 percent, considered a major correction.

After a nervous weekend, on Monday, mutual funds started dumping stocks in London before the American markets opened. It was October 19th, forever dubbed Black Monday in market lore. A deluge of futures selling hit Chicago at the opening bell, and within minutes, trading broke down in both Chicago and New York. Some big stocks did not get an opening price until 10:30. At one point, a portfolio insurer pumped out $100 million in thirteen futures sales orders over a space of just minutes. As futures went into free fall, buyers disappeared—like Askin's toxic waste, the futures effectively had no price. With panic spreading around the globe, New York exchange officials, for the first time, invoked "circuit breaker" rules to shut off trading, and there was serious talk of closing the exchanges. Stocks fell 23 percent in New York, the largest percentage drop in history. With no working links between stock and futures prices, the futures market fell even more.

The Fed responded with rivers of new money. (Gerald Corrigan, president of the New York Fed, reportedly had to apply severe pressure to New York banks to ensure that the new money would actually be used to support brokerages.) By week's end, order was more or less restored, and markets had staged a modest recovery, but some half-trillion in market wealth had been destroyed.

The market crash came shortly after Alan Greenspan took over as Fed chairman, and the Street gave him good marks for his quick response. At an FOMC (Federal Open Market

Committee) meeting two weeks after the crash, Greenspan was still very worried about the possibility of a global financial markets breakdown, although the Fed presidents thought that businesses in their districts had been relatively unaffected. Stock prices stabilized, but with a downward bias; by year's end, the P/E on the S&P 500 stocks was just under 15. That was a third lower than in August, but by historical standards still a healthy number.

What most impresses from the entire episode is the staggering fatuity of the idea of portfolio insurance, brilliant though the concept may have been. The strategy would work fine for a single firm, but if adopted by a whole market, it almost guarantees disaster. Leland and Rubinstein are obviously extremely smart men. Their firm, by some reports, managed half of all the portfolio insurance on the Street, or some $50 billion. It is astonishing that they didn't see the inevitable consequences of what they were doing.

Richard Bookstaber, who ran the portfolio insurance program at Morgan Stanley, recalls a conversation with a young salesman not long before Black Monday. The salesman wanted to confirm that Bookstaber was indeed managing some $3 billion in portfolio insurance; that if stocks started to fall, he would sell futures at steadily accelerating rates; and that at least twenty other big firms would do the same thing. Bookstaber confirmed that was all true. The young man invested his modest savings in market puts, which are options that pay handsomely in big downturns, and a few weeks later retired to a life of skiing.

The LTCM Crash

As a general rule, only the very smartest people can make truly catastrophic mistakes. Long-Term Capital Management (LTCM) was a hedge fund founded in 1993 by John Meriwether, a famed trader at Salomon. The glittering array of partners Meriwether assembled is a measure of the respect he commanded in finance circles. Besides his core Salomon team, the partners included Myron Scholes and Robert Merton, both of whom won the Nobel Prize in economics in 1997,* and David Mullins, a former vice chairman of the Fed.

Meriwether and his team were relative-value traders. They tracked price relationships between comparable instruments, looking for price divergences that their models said were unjustified. A standard example is the trading spread between on-the-run and off-the-run Treasury bonds. On-the-runs are the most recently issued bonds, and since they have more trading activity, they usually trade at slight premiums to older bonds. But the premium will disappear with time. So the trader shorts the on-the-run issue (sells bonds he doesn't own) and buys off-the-runs with the proceeds. By the time he closes out the transaction, prices normally will have moved back together, and he will make a small profit. Such arbitrage strategies are usually quite safe. It makes no difference if bond prices rise or fall, so long as the relative prices of the two

---

*The Black-Scholes formula is named for an article published by Scholes and Fischer Black in the *Journal of Political Economy* in 1973. Their model, as they always acknowledged, was substantially based on Merton's prior work. Black died in 1995, and the Nobel is not awarded posthumously.

move closer together. Occasionally, they don't, but Black-Scholes tells you those are rare occurrences.

Making serious money from the small margins in relative-value trading requires big positions and heavy leverage. Ten basis points (a tenth of a percent) on a $1 million position is only $1,000. But if you leverage up your position twenty-five times, the same deal returns 2.5 percent. (Because holding periods are typically short, the interest tab is small.) Doing a lot of those throughout the year can produce eye-popping returns, even if you're right only 80 percent to 90 percent of the time. The danger lies in all that leverage: When something goes wrong, it can go very wrong—as traders say, relative-value funds "eat like chickens and shit like elephants."

LTCM raised an extraordinary $1.25 billion in its investor offering and opened for business in 1994. Hoping to absorb some of Meriwether's trading technique, Merrill, Goldman, and a number of other firms lined up to provide leverage loans on extraordinarily generous terms, requiring little or no collateral, and demanding almost no information on LTCM's positions.

LTCM's launch coincided with the CMO crisis, which seriously roiled bond and mortgage markets, creating a candy store for relative-value traders. LTCM made a 20 percent return, mostly in bonds, in a year when bond markets were being hammered. Its returns in each of the next two years were more than 40 percent. The legend grew.

Problems started surfacing in 1997, when returns slipped to a pedestrian 17 percent. By then a number of other trading desks were emulating the LTCM strategy, and the increased presence of arbitrageurs necessarily narrowed profit opportunities. Meri-

wether sensibly concluded that LTCM was too big. The powerful growth in investor profits had ballooned LTCM's equity to
$7 billion. With leverage ratios typically in the 18–20 range,
that meant keeping more than $125 billion constantly deployed
in clever deals. At the end of the year, overriding howls of
protest, Meriwether forced outside investors to cash out a substantial portion of their holdings, shrinking LTCM's capital
base and upping his and his partners' stakes. It was the worst
trade he ever made. Some of the partners went deeply into debt
to finance their additional shares.

Hubris, along with the drive to improve yields, may have
been the real cause of LTCM's failure. The partners began to
drift away from their core disciplines into arenas in which
they had little experience, like currency trading and equity arbitrage (betting on takeovers), even as they steadily increased
leverage ratios.

Markets became extremely unsettled in mid-1998, with
currency collapses throughout Asia. Then Russia, which had
been a darling of Western investors, began to have trouble
servicing its external debt. Risk premiums soared—from
LTCM's perspective, the spreads between risky and safe
bonds, like U.S. Treasuries, became unusually wide. This was
LTCM's sweet spot, and it plunged as deeply as it possibly
could. As Western investors panicked, yields on Russian
Euro-bonds, which had once traded almost like investment-
grade instruments, shot up to 90 percent. The partners, and
their models, thought that was crazy, so they gorged on Russian bonds. Then in October, Russia effectively told its bond-
holders, and its own citizens, that they weren't going to pay
anybody, not even in rubles. And LTCM was dead.

The death spasm took a bit more than a month. Like David Askin's fund, the downward spiral could be mapped from collateral calls. Bear Stearns, again, was one of the first to move. Desperate for liquidity, Meriwether forced a consortium of banks to pony up against a never-drawn $500 million credit line, which was read as a sign of panic. In the meantime, corporate risk managers throughout Wall Street were forcing all the LTCM look-alikes to dump their positions, regardless of losses. LTCM alone could not sell; its positions were so big they would swamp the market. So the fund grimly held on, fending off margin calls as its capital shrank by hundreds of millions a day, waiting for its positions to turn. In his desperate trawl for new money, Meriwether enlisted the assistance of his friends at Goldman, which involved disclosing some of his positions. There are strong suspicions that Goldman traders used the information to trade against him.

The Federal Reserve did not formally intervene—a public agency can't visibly bail out a small coterie of multimillionaires. Instead, William McDonough, the president of the New York Fed, with Greenspan's approval, forced a rescue by LTCM's lenders. When Meriwether opened his books to Fed staff in late September, they were shocked. No one had imagined that LTCM had positions in excess of $100 billion, on an equity base that had shrunk to only $1 billion. LTCM was clearly insolvent and, at the rate its positions were exploding, would soon have no equity at all. At that point, there would be no choice but to dump all their holdings on the market, which, McDonough feared, might trigger a global meltdown.

After a week of rancorous discussions in the Fed board-room, twenty major commercial and investment banks agreed to pay in $3.65 billion to finance a takeover and workout of LTCM. The Fed helped as best it could by lowering interest rates. By the time LTCM was liquidated in 2000, the banks had recovered their investment, but little more. The partners lost an estimated $1.9 billion, and several were in serious financial difficulty. Such talented people, of course, could readily find new opportunities. Meriwether soon was raising new money and is now the general partner of JWM investors, a $2.6 billion hedge fund.

The Fed's intervention in the LTCM crisis was widely, and inaccurately, construed as a public bailout, although no taxpayer money was involved. The rescue capital all came from banks that had profited mightily from LTCM's business; McDonough, in effect, strongarmed them into disgorging some profits for the public good. None of the partners was poor after the workout, but most lost 90 percent or more of their wealth. That's more or less the way markets are supposed to work.

The more interesting question is posed by Martin Mayer, in his perceptive history of the Fed: Why, really, did the Fed force a settlement? Although the world largely accepted the party line that a disorderly failure would be violently disruptive, many remain skeptical. An equally plausible reason, perhaps, was to avoid a full airing of the *real* scandal: that at the very epicenter of American finance, a tiny group of people were able to borrow hundreds of billions of dollars from banks, and that neither the banks, nor the banks' regulators, had any idea of how much they had borrowed or what they were doing with it.

Geologic Shifts

Taken together, these three episodes illustrate the tectonic shifts in the financial markets of the 1980s and 1990s, and expose some of the seismic fault lines in the new terrain.

In the first place, all three of the crises developed in market pockets that were mostly outside the oversight of financial authorities. The relentless deregulation drive that started during the Reagan administration steadily shifted lending activities to the purview of nonregulated entities, until by 2006, only about a quarter of all lending occurred in regulated sectors, down from about 80 percent twenty years before.

Dogmatic market capitalists hailed the deregulation trend, none more enthusiastically than Alan Greenspan. In 1995, for example, Greenspan argued against margin—or minimum capital—rules on derivative positions. He claimed, implausibly, that a *lack* of margin requirements would "promote the safety and soundness of broker-dealers, by permitting more financing alternatives and, hence, more effective liquidity management." In the week before LTCM imploded, he told Congress, "Market pricing and counterparty surveillance can be expected to do most of the job of sustaining safety and soundness." And in 2003, he told an investment conference:

> Critics of derivatives often raise the specter of the failure of one dealer imposing debilitating losses on its counterparties, including other dealers, yielding a chain of defaults. However, derivative markets participants seem keenly aware of the counterparty credit risks associated with derivatives and take various measures to mitigate those risks.

Of course, this is the same Greenspan who told Congress that the Fed had to intervene in the LTCM crisis, because:

> Had the failure of LTCM triggered seizing up of markets, substantial damage could have been inflicted on many market participants, including some not directly involved with the firm, and could have potentially impaired the economies of many nations, including our own.

In other words, counterparty surveillance works fine, so long as you're willing to accept the occasional crash of "the economies of many nations." But given the enormous rewards that accrue to top-of-the-food-chain players like Meriwether, true market-believers may find that a cheap enough price.

A second fault line is a worsening of the "Agency" problem—or the problem of ensuring that an employee, a contractor, or a company performing a service doesn't act against your interest. A young trader named Nick Leeson destroyed Barings Bank in 1997 by taking exorbitant trading risks. By consensus, that was Barings' own fault. Highly compensated traders playing with the house's money are an extreme, and well-known, case of the Agency problem, so most trading houses have developed elaborate risk control procedures to protect themselves. Barings didn't, and paid for it.

Allaying customer Agency worries is the reason so many financial institutions advertise their interest in relationships. If they have a long-term relationship with you, the ads imply, they won't use their superior knowledge to cheat you. Their interests and yours are perfectly aligned.

The decomposition of mortgage banking that followed upon the success of the CMO greatly aggravated the Agency problem. When local S&Ls booked most new mortgages, their application clerks had every incentive to steer you to the best deal. Their institution expected to hold the mortgage for a long time, and the clerks may even have been your neighbors. But the new generation of mortgage banks sells off mortgages in weeks or months, brokers are usually compensated strictly from the fees they generate, and they often work with a customer entirely by e-mail or phone. Reports on Countrywide Financial, a very big lender caught up in the recent subprime mortgage fiasco, show staff steering customers toward products with the highest fees, even when much better alternatives are available. As financial machinery fragments, Agency problems abound; in the brave new world of absolute markets, it is not only dangerously naive to trust your mortgage broker, but based on recent scandals in college tuition lending, even your student aid counselor.

Finally, a third dangerous trend is the increased dominance of investment decisions by mathematical constructs. The mathematics of big portfolios analogizes price movements to models of heat diffusion and the motions of gas molecules, in which uncountable randomized micro-interactions lead to highly predictable macro-results. Although it's theoretically possible that all the air molecules in my room will shift to one corner, or that a torch applied to a metal bar will heat only one side, the laws of large numbers ensure that the actual frequency of such events is way beyond never.

Large securities portfolios usually do behave more or less as the mathematics suggest. But the analogies break down in times of stress. For shares truly to mirror gas molecules, trading would have to be costless, instantaneous, and continuous. In fact, it is lumpy, expensive, and intermittent. Trading is also driven by human choices that often make no sense in terms that models understand. Humans hate losing money more than they like making it. Humans are subject to fads. Even the most sophisticated traders exhibit herding behavior. Leland's and Rubinstein's portfolio insurance implicitly assumed that when their automated selling routines kicked in, buy-side computers would coolly apply options math to calculate rational purchase prices. But in real life, the buy-side was just a crowd of human traders screaming, "Holy s–! Everybody's selling like crazy! Dump everything!" In other words, as all three of this chapter's crises suggest, in real financial markets, air molecules have a disturbing knack for clumping on one side of the room.

Just before the LTCM crisis, the head of risk management at Merrill Lynch told me:

> The mathematicians tell you that a one-day 20 percent drop in equities happens how often—once every fifty years? And what about a $150 billion loss in S&Ls, or overnight yields of 1,000 percent in European currencies [1992], or a collapse in a major market like junk bonds? How often can those happen? Well, we've seen them all within just a few years. And if you're hedging Italian equities, what do you do when the market suddenly decides to close for five days, so there's no way of knowing what values are?

Residential mortgages became grist for quantitative portfolio management after they had been re-engineered into instruments that looked much like tradable bonds. The investment efficiencies generated large benefits for both investment banks and consumers but were quickly carried to dangerous extremes. Since that episode, however, there has been an all-out push to reconfigure almost all assets—office building mortgages, emerging market bonds, risky bank loans, and much else—so they will behave more like idealized securities rather than the lumpy, gnarly instruments they really are. The re-engineering greatly improved market efficiencies and reduced funding costs but also created the illusion that the underlying risks were well understood and under control.

All three of those trends—the shift of financial transactions to unregulated markets, the steady worsening of the Agency problem, and the pretense that all of finance can be mathematized—flowed together to create the great credit bubble of the 2000s.

CHAPTER 4

A Wall of Money

The early 2000s were a nervous, quarrelsome, time—terrorism, airport check-in lines, a discouraging war, energy disruption, nasty politics. But to be a banker, or a high-rolling investor, was very heaven.

When the dot-com boom imploded in late 2000, the Fed responded by cutting the federal funds rate from 6.5 percent to 3.5 percent within the space of just a few months. In the aftermath of the tragic events of September 11, 2001, the Fed continued to lower rates—all the way down to 1 percent by 2003, the lowest rate in a half-century. The Fed did not start raising rates again until mid-2004, and for thirty-one consecutive months, the base inflation-adjusted short-term interest rate was *negative*. For bankers, in other words, money was free.

Worries over thin capitalization at large banks in the late 1980s prompted the regulators of all major countries to impose much tougher bank capital rules. Bankers would become more discriminating in their credit decisions, the reasoning went, if they had more capital at risk on each loan. The bankers, however, had seen how residential mortgage bankers could run booming lending businesses with only wisps of capital. The secret was securitization—packaging up loans in the form of collateralized mortgage obligations (CMOs) and selling them off to pension funds and other investors. When the new capital rules started to bite in the mid-1990s, therefore, banks embraced securitization. Instead of holding their commercial mortgages, corporate loans, high-yield takeover loans, emerging market loans, and such on their books, the way bankers always had done, they began to package them up as collateralized loan obligations (CLOs) or collateralized debt obligations (CDOs) and sell them to outside investors. They could still collect hefty fees while encumbering little if any of their capital. Lending, in other words, was becoming costless.

For many years there has been an active bank-to-bank trading market in derivatives that help balance banks' currency and interest-rate positions. A new class of credit derivatives was developed in the 1990s that purportedly insured banks against loan defaults. Although the details differ, the basic idea is much like that of the portfolio insurance made famous by the 1987 stock market crash. Banks became enthusiastic consumers of credit insurance, as did the investors buying the loans that banks were securitizing. And just as in 1987, the availability of credit insurance let investors climb higher and higher up the risk curve. Lulled by the presence of credit insurance, investors who might have been wary of the lowest rated CLOs and CDOs snapped them up for their extra yields. And why not? The mathematicians had banished risk.

When money is free, and lending is costless and riskless, the rational lender will keep on lending until there is no one else to lend to. Alan Greenspan foresaw a glorious new era of finance. Adding to his string of memorable bubble endorsements, he announced "a new paradigm of active credit management."

Even the most unglamorous drudge-shops in the gleaming towers of finance chunked out unending streams of gold. Home equity loans to strapped homeowners, high-rate credit cards for insolvent consumers, all became fair game. You logged in the loans, collected your fees, and sold them off to yield-hungry investors. The investors were "insured." Your fees were real money. The loans might even be paid off.

The leveraged-buyout business, after a highbrow restyling as private equity, came roaring back. A typical deal: Put up $1 billion, borrow $4 billion more, snap up a healthy company for $5 billion (after making a very rich deal with its executives), vote yourselves a "special dividend" of $1 billion, then as the buyout-fueled stock market keeps rising, sell the company back to the public, pocketing another couple billion, all the while taking *no* risk. "People talk about a wall of money," one banker said. Private equity funds didn't have to raise capital; it was chasing them.

All bubbles pop, and the longer they expand, the worse the implosion. By late fall 2007, the hiss of escaping bubble gas had turned into a roar. But before we look at the Great Unwinding that is under way, we need first to unpack the key developments that blew up the credit bubble to such a perilous size.

The "Greenspan Put"

William McChesney Martin served as chairman of the Federal Reserve for eighteen years, spanning presidential administrations from Truman through Nixon. It was Martin, probably more than anyone, who established the standard definition of the Fed's role as "leaning against the wind"—easing credit in hard times and tightening it before expansions got frothy. Since political pressures almost always line up on the side of easing, Martin himself tended to stress the tightening: "The function of the Federal Reserve is to take away the punch bowl just as the party is getting good."

Now follow the interplay between the interest rate actions of the Greenspan FOMC (Federal Open Market Committee) and real economic growth. Before the 9/11 attacks, the funds rate was already down to 3.5 percent. Immediately after the attack, the FOMC pushed it down in four quick steps to 1.75 percent by year-end and held it there through most of 2002. Economic growth was dismal in the last half of 2001, of course, but recovered to a respectable, if somewhat anemic, 2.4 percent annualized rate during the first three quarters of 2002.

In November 2002, amid distinct signs that the economy was slowing sharply, the Fed made a very aggressive half-point cut in the funds rate, taking it down to only 1.25 percent. Growth stayed sluggish in the last quarter of 2002 and the first quarter of 2003 but picked up strongly in the next quarter, in part due to the Bush tax cuts and the surge in Iraq-related spending. At the FOMC meeting at the end of that quarter, however, the committee imposed yet another cut in the funds rate to only 1 percent, the lowest since 1954. The next quarter's growth jumped to an "extraordinary" (the committee's word) 7.5 percent annual rate before settling down to a solid mid–3 percent rate for the rest of 2003 and through 2004. But the committee stuck with the 1 percent funds rate for a full year, before starting the measured series of quarter-point funds rate increases that finally leveled out at 5.25 percent in early 2006. In contrast to Martin's dictum, it appears, the FOMC chose to keep refilling the punch bowl until it was sure the party was really under way.

Even more controversial is Greenspan's resolute insistence on focusing only on consumer price inflation, while ignoring signs of rampant inflation in the price of *assets*, especially houses and bonds of all kinds. Academics can adduce technical reasons why central banks should not concern themselves with asset prices. But common sense demands some intervention when prices of a major asset class are soaring beyond all reason. In 2004, for example, the *Economist* magazine worried that "the global financial system . . . has become a giant money press as American's easy-money policy has spilled beyond its borders. . . . This gush of global liquidity has not pushed up inflation. Instead, it has flowed into share prices and houses around the world, inflating a series of asset-price bubbles." Stephen Roach, chairman of Morgan Stanley Asia, has called the Fed's performance during this period "unconscionable."

Europeans were more restrained in their criticisms, at least in public. One can almost hear the polite coughing in a policy study, "Asset Price Bubbles and Monetary Policy," released by the European Central Bank in the spring of 2005:

> The close association between potentially disruptive asset-price booms and excess credit and liquidity creation is particularly important for central banks. . . . Indeed, certain historical episodes suggest that major asset-price escalations can be encouraged by lax monetary conditions which are not immediately reflected in an increase in consumer price inflation. . . .
>
> [A]s households are typically encouraged to spend out of their capital gains when asset prices advance, durable and sizeable bubbles can boost consumer expenditure. . . . In this respect, empirical evidence tends to suggest that a deflating bubble in the housing market is more costly than an equally sized crash in the stock market, as housing equity is more widespread and more intensely used as collateral for securing credit.

An alternative title for the study might have been "Earth to Federal Reserve: Please Stop!"

The term "Greenspan Put" became commonplace around Wall Street in the early 2000s. A "put" is an option that allows the owner to sell an asset to some third party at a fixed price, no matter what. These excerpts from an influential investment newsletter from August 2007 perfectly capture the import of the Greenspan Put:

> I remember well the stock market crash of October 1987. . . . There were widespread fears that the big banks might be in trouble and that a credit crunch would follow. . . . In response,

the Fed cut interest rates three times in six weeks. The U.S. economy continued to grow . . . stocks recovered to new highs. . . .

The 1998 stock market plunge saw the S&P 500 dive. [He describes the Asian currency crisis, LTCM fiasco, and the Russian default] . . . [O]f course we were headed for serious recession. In response, *the Fed cut rates three times in seven weeks.* . . . In 1999 and 2000, the U.S. and global economies recorded their strongest growth in a decade. . . .

The 2001 recession, worsened by the 9/11 attacks, sparked many of the concerns we are hearing today about a credit crunch. As a result, *the Fed cut rates three times in seven weeks.* There was no serious credit crunch.

That is the Greenspan Put: No matter what goes wrong, the Fed will rescue you by creating enough cheap money to buy you out of your troubles.

But there are practical limits to how far the Fed can go. Only one Fed chairman presided over a longer period of negative interest rates than Greenspan did. That was Arthur Burns, who set the dubious record of thirty-seven months during the Nixon-Ford-Carter years of 1974–77. But we know how that story ended. It took Paul Volcker, a nasty recession, and a decade of very high interest rates to repair the damage.

The Greatest Real Estate Bubble in World History

From 2000 until mid-2005, America experienced a housing boom—part of a global real estate bubble that Yale University's Robert Shiller, who has made a career of studying housing booms, has pronounced the greatest in history. The market value of homes grew by more than 50 percent, and there was a frenzy of new construction. Merrill Lynch estimated that about half of all American GDP growth in the first half of 2005 was housing-related, either directly through home-building and housing-related purchases, like new furniture, or indirectly, by spending refinancing cash flows. More than half of all new private-sector jobs since 2001, they calculated, were in housing-related activities.

Most Americans might be surprised to learn that over the long term, home prices track very closely to the rate of inflation. We regard them as such a reliable source of savings because a house is usually our only highly leveraged asset. Buy a $100,000 house, put 20 percent down, and finance the rest with a conventional fixed-rate mortgage. In twenty-five years, at 2 percent inflation, the house is worth about $168,000, and you own it free and clear. On the reasonable assumption that mortgage and maintenance expenses are about the same as renting, you've made a compounded annual return on your initial equity of almost 9 percent. For most families, it is the best investment they ever make.

But a 50 percent price jump in five years changes attitudes. Buy a $200,000 house with 90 percent financing, which was available to anyone, sell out at $300,000 five years later, and you've quintupled your initial equity investment. Use half of your profit for a 10 percent down payment on a $500,000 home and wait for it to happen again. Those are exciting numbers.

Why did it happen? Housing booms are usually triggered by demographics. The suburbanization shift of the 1950s reflected deep-rooted changes in family dynamics, as if Americans had collectively decided to compensate for the low birthrates of the 1930s and 1940s. A quarter-century later, their grown-up children, and America's vast internal migration toward the Southeast and Southwest, drove the real estate boom of the 1970s and 1980s.

But the demographics of the 1990s were pretty dull. Even the boomers had finally hit the age when people mostly stay put. The economy did well, of course, but the most spectacular gains were concentrated in elite enclaves on the two coasts. The median real household wage was basically flat, and consumer savings were at historic lows—not the stuff of real estate booms.

The 2000s real estate bubble may be one of those rare beasts conjured into the world solely by financiers, which is confirmed by the fact that housing bubbles also occurred in the United Kingdom, Australia, Spain, and other countries where residential lending became unusually loose.

Since houses are so leveraged, their prices are hypersensitive to changes in interest rates. As long-term rates trended steadily downward in the second half of the 1990s, the big banks plunged headlong into the refinancing, or "refi," business. It took a couple of years for consumers to catch on—extracting money from your house was an exotic concept. Banks mounted lavish advertising campaigns to stoke their enthusiasm. Refis jumped from $14 billion in 1995 to nearly a quarter-trillion in 2005, the great majority of them resulting in higher loan amounts. Lower interest rates let you borrow more for the same monthly payment, pay off your old loan, and buy a new car with the difference. By the 2000s, consumers had learned how to ride down the interest-rate curve with abandon, many of them going back to the well again and again.

To keep up with the surge of paperwork, banks and the swelling ranks of thinly capitalized mortgage banks re-engineered the application and approval process. Automated credit scoring speeded up application reviews. Trimming back on documentation brought more borrowers into the fold. Tracking appraiser performance pressured appraisers to conform their values to a bank's mortgage targets. Automated underwriting software allowed much higher loan-to-income ratios. There was a proliferation of new "affordability products"—devices to make housing more available to marginal credits, most of which were strongly supported by community advocates. They included varieties of adjustable-rate mortgages, or ARMs, to let consumers lock in their expectation of continuously falling rates; piggyback loans to finance the down payments and closing expenses for savings-poor buyers; and more emphasis on subprime loans, or higher-rate and higher-fee products for borrowers who did not meet the traditional lending tests. Lenders also welcomed "flippers"— people buying houses solely for the purpose of reselling in a year or so. By 2005, 40 percent of all home purchases were either for investment or as second homes. (Experts believe that a large share of the "second homes" actually are speculations for resale; lenders don't review vacation-home purchases as closely as investment properties.)

As always, Greenspan cheered it on. In 2004, when families had a historic chance to lock in long-term fixed-rate mortgages at only 5.5 percent, Greenspan said they were losing "tens of thousands of dollars" by not grabbing one-year

ARMs, then at teaser rates of only 3.25 percent. In any scrap-book of bad advice from economic gurus, that should be near the top of the list. Greenspan's fellow Federal Reserve gover-nor, the late Edward Gramlich, also reported that Greenspan had no interest in looking into growing signs of predatory be-havior in the subprime industry.

Most financial booms have positive effects, and this one was no exception. The national rate of home ownership in-creased from the roughly 64 percent that prevailed through-out the 1980s and early 1990s, all the way up to 69 percent by 2005. Home ownership tends to stabilize communities, lay a solid base for family finances, and inculcate habits of thrift and planning in children. The new entrants to ownership ranks were disproportionately black and Latino families, fi-nally getting a piece of the American dream.

But, again like most booms, it inevitably veered into de-structive excess. By 2003 or so, mortgage lenders were run-ning out of people they could plausibly lend to. Instead of curtailing lending, they spread their nets to vacuum up prospects with little hope of repaying their loans. Subprime lending jumped from an annual volume of $145 billion in 2001 to $625 billion in 2005, more than 20 percent of total issuances. More than a third of subprime loans were for 100 percent of the home value—even more when the fees were added in. Light-documentation mortgages transmuted into "ninja" loans—no income, no job, no assets.

The industry's underbelly became viciously predatory: A mortgage might include several different loans at teaser rates that quickly reset to double or triple the initial rates. The new monthly payments frequently were higher than the borrower's total income. "Negative amortizations" were loans with initial payments that didn't cover interest, but the unpaid interest was added to the principal at killer rates. Gross overcharges for fees and brokerage were buried in the loan principal. The standard lender escrow accounts to ensure the payment of taxes and insurance were eliminated. Borrowers thought their monthly payments were smaller and quickly defaulted on insurance and tax payments. "Yield spread premium" fees for brokers were bonuses for originating high-rate loans for borrowers who qualified for better deals.

Angelo Mozilo, the billionaire financier who built Countrywide Financial into the nation's largest residential mortgage lender, blames the woes in the subprime market on aggressive borrowers and advocates for the poor, who forced banks to be more accommodating toward lower-income families.

Well, maybe. In New York City in 2005 and 2006, however, black "affinity marketing" mortgage brokers fanned out through the poorer areas, targeting homeowners with substantial equity in their homes. Edward Jordan, a seventy-eight-year-old retired postal worker, has owned his home since 1975 and was just a few years from paying off his mortgage. He was approached by a broker who told him that he was overpaying; she could get him a rate of only 1 percent. Jordan sought out another broker, who confirmed that that was so, and placed a mortgage for him with Countrywide. Total fees were $20,000.

After the deal was closed, Jordan, who had trusted the brokers, discovered that the interest rate would quickly escalate to as high as 9.95 percent. When he complained to Country-wide, the firm's loss-mitigation group offered him an interest-only alternative, but at a higher rate, and with steadily escalating principal, so monthly payments would eventually rise to several times Jordan's income. Jordan, who lives solely on his pension, is now afraid he will lose his home. He also happens to have a credit score of 800, which places him among the 13 percent best credit risks in the nation. On any construction of the deal, he was robbed by Countrywide. The files of the legal services organization in the area where Jordan lives are bulging with cases like these. And the most active lenders were the big national players, like Countrywide, New Century (now bankrupt), and Fremont General.

And it's not just the poor. A surprising number of subprimes went to affluent people who were stretching for bubble-priced homes or second homes that they will not be able to afford if the economy turns down. There has never been a starker demonstration of the Agency problem—if loan originators have no stake in a borrower's continued solvency, the competition for fees will inevitably degrade the average quality of loans.

As of the end of 2007, the industry borders on catastrophe. The housing boom is over: The widely followed Case-Shiller index of home resales shows that real home prices have fallen steadily throughout 2007. (As late as 2006, the forecasting consensus was that house prices never fall.) Chasing the numbers down, most economists now anticipate a real national price drop in the 10 percent range, although outside estimates are creeping toward 30 percent.

Pessimism is fully warranted. Some $350 billion worth of subprime and near-subprime loans closed in 2005 and 2006 will reset, most at much higher interest rates over the next two years or so. Delinquencies have been rising rapidly and, given the very low quality of recent-vintage loans, can only accelerate. Widespread foreclosures and vacancies can have devastating effects on poorer neighborhoods—research suggests that values drop within radii measured in miles. Lender bankruptcies, with their attendant legal tangles, are spreading among the industry's erstwhile roman-candle growth stars. Countrywide itself averted bankruptcy by dint of a $2 billion bailout by Bank of America, but its stock has continued to slide since the bailout. Drying up of cash-flow refis is already having a major effect on consumers' ability to carry on spending.

As the subprime crisis developed through the spring and summer of 2007, the unanimous response of the wise men of finance was that it was containable. Subprime and similarly risky mortgages, like undocumented "Alt-A" loans and much of the home equity second-lien market, despite their recent prominence, still account for no more than 15 to 20 percent of all outstanding mortgages. Even assuming a high rate of delinquencies within that group, in the context of a $12 trillion economy, it looks like small potatoes.

It's not. What makes it so important, and so devastating, is not its absolute size, but the way lower-quality mortgages have marbled their way through the entire world's credit system—and they are just one of several big, and very shaky, asset classes to have done so. Examining how that could happen takes us to the heart of the giant credit bubble that we have so willy-nilly constructed.

The Great Game of Risk Transfer

We saw in the last chapter how Wall Street re-engineered residential mortgage portfolios into structured bonds called collateralized mortgage obligations (CMOs). A portfolio of mortgages would be dedicated to support the issuance of a family of bonds. The bonds would be tiered in horizontal slices, or tranches, and portfolio cash flows were preferentially directed to the top tranches. Since the top tranches had first claim on cash flows, they qualified for the highest investment-grade ratings. The bottom tranches absorbed all initial defaults but paid high yields. The mix of very high-quality, high-rated instruments plus a smaller quantity of high-yield, high-risk paper matched up well with the preferences of long-term investors. Wall Street inevitably pushed the tranching technology to an extreme, triggering a serious mortgage market crash in 1994. After 1996 or so, as the market recovered, more conservatively structured (and renamed) residential mortgage-backed securities (RMBS) gradually became a standard element in most big investor portfolios.

The advent of CMBS, or commercial mortgage-backed securities, was a conceptual breakthrough pioneered by the federal agency charged with selling off the multibillions of commercial mortgages acquired from failed S&Ls. Unlike residential mortgages, commercial mortgages are individually tailored to their underlying assets and don't readily lend themselves to pooling. The solution was to involve the rating agencies in the construction of the pool. Banks would assemble a detailed profile for each property in a projected pool—its financials, management, tenant history, maintenance records, and mortgage details. The rating agencies used proprietary models to estimate default risk and actively negotiated the pool structure—rejuggling properties to improve geographic diversity, or insisting on more buildings with long-term, blue-chip tenants. A typical CMBS had five or six tranches, although more recent structures have many more, and might include 150 buildings with face-value mortgages in the $10 million range and up. Just as with RMBS, CMBS broadened the investor base for commercial mortgages and visibly tightened interest spreads.

The floodgates were opened. So long as you did the gritty, credit-by-credit documentation work with the rating agencies, you could securitize anything. Companies started selling asset-backed securities (ABS) to finance equipment, transportation fleets, or anything else investors could value. GE was an early and creative ABS issuer. Investment banks created collateralized bond obligations (CBOs), while commercial banks experimented with collateralized loan obligations (CLOs). (CDOs, or collateralized debt obligations, became the generic name for all types of securitized assets, including mortgages.) In almost all cases, a trust, or special-purpose entity (SPE), technically independent of the parent, would be created to purchase the assets. The purchase would be financed by selling securitized paper, usually with a tranched structure to broaden investor appeal. For banks, selling assets and liabilities off their balance sheets reduces strain on regulatory capital; for companies, it lowers apparent debt.

Then it got more complicated. About the same time as the securitized, or structured, finance industry was evolving at a breakneck pace, some brilliant financial engineers introduced new families of credit derivatives, the most important of which is the credit default swap. To take a simple case: Suppose US Bank decides it is underexposed to credits in Southeast Asia. The old way to fix that was to buy some Asian bank branches or partner with a local bank. A credit default swap short-circuits the process. For a fee, US Bank will guarantee against any losses on a loan portfolio held by Asia Bank and will receive the interest and fees on those loans. Asia Bank will continue to service the loans, so its local customers will see no change, but Asia Bank, in Street jargon, will have purchased insurance for its risk portfolio, freeing up regulatory capital for business expansion. Credit default swaps became one of the fastest-growing new financial instruments ever. The notional value of credit default swaps—that is, the size of portfolios covered by credit default agreements—grew from $1 trillion in 2001 to $45 trillion by mid-2007.

Just as credit default swaps made it easy for a bank to diversify its geographic risk, they could also replicate credits across a range of risk classes, much like the tranches of a CDO. With powerful computers and a lot of brainpower, a CDO manager can create a synthetic CDO, that is, an array of swaps with a risk structure just like a normal "cash-flow" CDO that is built from real securities. The manager must carefully build a reference CDO portfolio, mirroring thousands of real market instruments, and then model its performance under stress. When he is satisfied with the structure, he creates the family of credit default swaps that will return the same profits and losses as the bonds on an identical cash-flow CDO. What makes synthetics attractive for CDO managers is that they avoid the logistics and financial risk of buying in and warehousing securities while a CDO is being constructed and sold. In 2006 and the first part of 2007, the volume of new synthetics outstripped the volume of new cash-flow CDOs.

CDO managers are typically subsidiaries of financial services conglomerates—the largest 2006 issuer, for example, TCW Inc., is an American subsidiary of the French bank Société Générale. Total issuance of new cash-flow and synthetic CDOs and CLOs in 2006 was about $600 billion, with an average deal size of $900 million, and total outstandings of about $1.5 trillion. Before the market freeze that hit in mid-2007, the strong volume of issuances had brought total outstandings to about $2 trillion. The importance of synthetics is that their issuance volume is not constrained by the volume of underlying reference securities. In other words, the sum of subprime mortgages in both cash-flow and synthetic CDOs could easily be larger than the volume in the real world, but investors will reap exactly the same gains and suffer exactly the same losses from the synthetics as from the real ones.

The boom in CDO issuance was well under way by year-end 2003. With negative real American interest rates, investors were keen on opportunities to improve yield. Japanese rates were even lower, at essentially zero, so a large yen-to-dollar "carry trade" developed, whereby investors would borrow yen, convert them to dollars, and invest in risky American instruments. Most big banks and asset managers created CDO shops, while private equity firms like Blackstone and KKR set up CDO subsidiaries of their own to offload debt from their takeover deals.

Riskier loans were actually preferred by CDO managers since the higher yields offer greater flexibility in building out a structure. (There is enough yield left over after the triple-A tranche is constructed to create highly marketable lower-tier bonds.) With CDO shops eager for product, it made market sense for the Countrywides of the world to maximize their fee income by focusing on the riskiest mortgages. Leveraged corporate loans developed their own category of subprimes, so-called Lite Model loans, which included "asset-lites" and "covenant-lites" that stripped away most of the traditional protection for investors. Commercial and investment banks were happy to finance high-risk Lite Model loans in the expectation that they would be sloughed off onto CLO investors.

Rating agencies did their part to feed the enthusiasm. The public may think of them as detached arbiters of security quality, like a financial Supreme Court. In fact, they were building booming, diversified, high-margin businesses. Between 2002 and 2006, for instance, Moody's doubled its revenue and more than tripled its stock price. Their core customers, however, were the big banks and investment banks, and since CDO bond ratings were usually heavily negotiated, it seems clear that the agencies slanted their ratings to please their clients.

High CDO bond ratings are often excused by reference to the very low default rates of the era. But default rates were *not* low. From mid-2000 through mid-2002, subprime mortgages in foreclosure hovered around 9 percent. Over the four years from 2000 through 2003, default rates on high-yield corporate bonds averaged about 8 percent, with a high of almost 13 percent in 2002, the highest rate ever. Structured bond assets, an early version of the CDO, also flamed out badly during the same period.

Very low default rates didn't kick in until the flood of easy credit from the Greenspan free-money policy had time to work its way through the economy. That took until the end of 2003 or so, when the CDO market was already taking off. By 2006, high-yield bond default rates were indeed historically low—when markets are rising and money is free, it's easy to borrow your way out of a crunch. But it is obviously irresponsible to treat a couple years of unusual performance as the new norm. The rating agencies doled out all those investment-grade ratings, in short, not because their models were hostage to recent history, but because they strenuously ignored it.

In the boom years of 2005 and 2006, probably 80 percent of the securities in CDOs were mortgage-backeds, possibly 70 percent of those were below top-grade, and at least half were subprime or second-lien home equity lines—and these were the same years the industry was pumping out some of the most egregiously irresponsible loans in history. By assuming a permanent new era of very low defaults, it was possible to build families of bonds such that 80 percent of the issued bonds had triple-A and double-A ratings, even though 70 percent of the supporting assets were subprime. Analysts call this phenomenon "embedded leverage." The CDO analyst Janet Tavakoli cites two apparently identical offerings of triple-A-rated CDO bonds supported in part by subprime mortgages. A 2 percent default rate in one portfolio would require that 2 percent of the triple-A bonds be downgraded.

The same default rate in the second portfolio would require that *40 percent* of the bonds be downgraded.* Few investors can perform such analyses, or even think of looking beyond the triple-A label. Subprime mortgages, moreover, come with such a variety of terms—fixed going to floating, second liens, negative interest, and the like—that they are extremely hard to model to begin with.

To complicate matters, CDO managers often freely mix instrument types, so any bond might be backed by a grab bag of subordinated claims on a mélange of risky assets. Leverage is compounded further with "CDO^{2}s," or CDOs of CDOs. You collect the risky tranches of a number of CDOs, which can sometimes be the hardest to place, and use them to support a new CDO, with a range of high-to-low risk-rated tranches. Highly rated bonds magically materialize out of a witches' soup of very smoky stuff. There is even a smattering of "CDO^{3}s" out there, or CDOs built from the leftover tranches of CDO^{2}s. Very big, very complex, very opaque structures built on extremely rickety foundations are a recipe for collapse.

---

* The difference results from the fact that portfolios with the same average risk may contain quite different distributions of risky instruments. If a portfolio has a "U-shaped" distribution, with a small number of very high-risk bonds and the rest of quite good quality, defaults in the lower tranches would have minimal implications for the remainder. If the bonds are clustered much closer in quality, however, defaults in the lower tranches could be expected to ripple through the portfolio much more quickly. Portfolios of apparently similar riskiness, therefore, might behave much differently under stress. The risk shifts are also likely to be nonlinear—they move in jumps rather than smoothly—which makes them very difficult to model correctly.

Seams Start to Show

In June 2007, equity markets were roaring ahead, despite a persistent undercurrent of nervousness in bond markets. Then two Bear Stearns hedge funds that invested primarily in mortgage-backeds announced that they were having trouble meeting margin calls. The funds were run by Ralph Cioffi, one of Wall Street's longtime mortgage-backed gurus, and possessor of an exceptional funds-management track record. Like many outperforming asset managers, he was highly leveraged. Although he had invested primarily in higher-rated CDOs, by external indices their value had dropped from near 100 to the mid-90s. That's sizeable for highly rated bonds, and since Cioffi was leveraged about 17:1, he took a big paper loss.

After the writedown, the securities in Cioffi's prime brokers' margin accounts no longer covered their lending exposures. Merrill Lynch, which had most of the exposure, asked for an additional $145 million in cash or good securities, which Cioffi didn't have. Not a problem for Merrill: It held most of Cioffi's securities and had the right to sell whatever was necessary to meet the margin agreements. Two weeks of tense boardroom confrontations ensued. At one point Merrill seized $845 million worth of securities only to discover that nobody wanted them—shades of David Askin and LTCM. Bear Stearns, which technically had no legal responsibility for the funds, reluctantly stumped up $3.2 billion to close out its positions and of course fired Cioffi. (Merrill's harshness, rumor has it, was in part tit-for-tat for Bear's role in precipitating the 1994 CMO crisis and its refusal to pony up its share of the LTCM settlement.)

Then the world discovered how deeply American sub-prime paper had infiltrated global finance. The roster of blue-chip financial companies admitting to big losses included Nomura, the Royal Bank of Scotland, Lehman Bros., Credit Suisse, and Deutschebank. France's BNP Paribas had three big investment funds that it could no longer value. Two large Australian hedge funds closed their doors. Commerzbank and IKB Deutsche Industrie Bank announced big write-downs, and IKB had to bail out its asset management unit, Rhinelander Funding. A U.K. hedge fund manager, Caliber, went into liquidation, while the Bank of England had to bail out Northern Rock, one of the country's largest mortgage lenders. Even China was taking losses.

Two other events in the fall of 2007 further limned the outlines of an evolving slow-motion crisis. Banks competed for their share of the white-hot private equity business by providing up-front deal financing, or bridge financing, which they would lay off later through CDOs and CLOs. By rough count, the top banks had committed to some $300 billion to $400 billion in bridges for private equity deals that were still being finalized when the subprime debacle hit the front pages. CDO and CLO financing stopped cold, and the banks started squirming. Some deals were killed outright, and others were bargained down. (We will come back to private equity in Chapter 6.) The world will not be worse off, of course, if fewer private equity deals get done, but the episode suggests the critical role CDOs have played in maintaining the flood of liquidity.

The second event is to the same point but is much scarier. Commercial paper is a standard form of note for interbank and intercompany short-term borrowing. It is issued for short durations, so notes from top-drawer banks normally trade at a microscopic margin above the overnight Fed funds rate or its London equivalent, LIBOR. But in early September, rates on so-called asset-backed commercial paper (ABCP) sold by major banks suddenly spiked up nearly 20 percent (from 5+ percent to 6+ percent).

In addition to the multitrillion CDO and synthetic CDO market, it emerged, there is a kind of shadow CDO world called SIVs,* or structured investment vehicles, run within— but legally separate from—the major money center banks. SIVs are typically Cayman Island limited partnerships that collect bundles of bank loans or other securities. They are especially convenient for moving assets off a bank's balance sheet and apparently have substantial holdings of commercial and residential mortgages and mortgage-backed securities. (At this writing, nearly three months after the SIV crisis hit, the holdings still are not clear.)

To squeeze out extra profit, banks chose not to fund their SIVs with equivalent maturity debt. Instead, they financed them with inexpensive ABCP, usually issued in three-month maturities. Total asset-backed commercial paper outstandings were about $1.2 trillion, so the banks were regularly rolling over that amount in the money markets. About a third of it, apparently, was specifically for SIVs. The September rate spike, dubbed a buyer's strike by the *Financial Times*, was a

---

* "SIV" is an infelicitous choice of labels, for it is more widely known as the acronym for the simian immunodeficiency virus (affecting apes and monkeys) that mutated into HIV and AIDS.

shout from buyers that "We don't trust you and don't know what you're doing with our money." A number of money market funds were caught in the backdraft. ABCP from top banks is a standard money market fund holding, and some sponsors have had to stump up money so their fund shares don't dip below the sacred $1 value.

By late November, the world of SIVs was approaching a state of chaos. Outstanding interbank commercial paper balances had dropped below $900 billion, with most of the falloff due to refusal to refinance SIVs, leaving banks potentially on the hook to supply more than $300 billion of very risky, quite unexpected, financings. A *Financial Times* review disclosed that at banks like Citi and J. P. Morgan Chase, drawings under SIV and other captive liquidity lines were growing very rapidly. At Citi, the lending to its own SIVs was more than three times higher than its net new global consumer lending. The rating agency Moody's also announced that it would undertake a broad review of outstanding SIV paper, reporting that many SIV managers "have told us they now do not expect the SIV model to survive in its current form." A number of SIVs, particularly in Europe, have already been liquidated.

A consortium of American banks, led, or possibly strong-armed, by Citi with the cooperation of the Treasury, is attempting to organize a super-SIV to take $75 billion to $100 billion in SIV loans off their books. The usefulness, and even the plausibility, of such an exercise is diminishing by the day. More and more, it looks like a last-gasp effort to defer recognition of losses. At the end of November, HSBC began a "restructuring" of its two SIVs, with the apparent intention of bringing $45 billion of SIV assets onto its own balance sheet, which would almost certainly entail substantial writedowns. The forthrightness of HSBC's solution may put further pressure on the American banks to take a similar step.

The extreme leveraging in the financial sector started to come undone in October, when the big banks and investment banks reported some $20 billion in losses, $11 billion of it at Citi and Merrill, primarily in subprime-based CDOs. The first reaction was relief that the banks were finally coming clean. But within just a couple weeks, banks revised their loss estimates to more than $45 billion, including recalculations of the third quarter and new losses in October. Some $20 billion was at Citi and Merrill. Merrill's CEO, Stan O'Neal, was fired, and Citi's Chuck Prince resigned. Since Citi is almost certainly facing further writedowns on at least the same scale in the fourth quarter, analysts began to fear for the bank's capital adequacy. The bank earned a temporary respite with an emergency $7.5 billion capital infusion from Abu Dhabi, in the form of a convertible bond with a punishing "subjunk" 11 percent interest coupon.

As of late November, the market bottom is rapidly receding into an endless black hole. I will estimate probable losses in Chapter 6. But to appreciate the scale of the unwinding that is to come, we need some more context.

The discussion of the structured finance boom to this point has left out one critical set of players. As the CMO crash of 1994 illustrated, the limiting factor on CDO-type securities is finding a buyer for the toxic waste, the bottom tranches, or the equity that absorbs all of a CDO's first losses. The buyers for CDO toxic waste serve as a kind of global securitization risk sink, the foundation that keeps the huge, wobbly struc-ture still standing. Who can absorb that much risk? We'll ex-plore that in Chapter 6 because it will greatly influence the course of the Great Unwinding that is getting under way.

Another important prior question is, why isn't the Fed stepping in much more aggressively? What has happened to the Greenspan, or Bernanke, Put?

The sad fact is that there isn't much the Fed can do. All the years of working the liquidity pump has sucked out every-thing but the brine. The "wall of money" that has kept Amer-ican markets afloat also created a global dollar tsunami that has left a waterlogged world in its wake. That's the subject of the next chapter.

A Tsunami of Dollars

Seigniorage was the collection of rights possessed by a feudal lord over his tenants, including, tradition has it, first dibs on bedding the peasant girls on their wedding nights. In the realm of money, the term referred to the sovereign's ability to debase his coinage. By setting the value of coins somewhat higher than the precious metal they contained, he made a profit on each coin. Seigniorage in the modern era refers to the persistent overvaluation of a reserve currency. When France's Charles de Gaulle complained bitterly of dollar seigniorage in the 1960s, however, he was thinking more in terms of lords forcing themselves on young maidens, for Americans were exploiting their privileged position by taking over French industry on the cheap.

The American dollar's status as the world's reserve currency was officially confirmed by the Bretton Woods agreements after World War II. Reestablishing functioning currencies was a first-order priority for reviving the economies of war-ravaged countries. But the hyperinflation of the intrawar years had made people suspicious of paper money. If central banks supported their currency issues with substantial dollar reserves, however, citizens could be confident that their francs or yen or deutschemarks would retain their values. The value of the dollar, in turn, was fixed by the long-standing commitment to redeem dollars for gold at the rate of $35 per ounce. Virtually all prices in international trade were set in dollars.

But the privilege of seigniorage has a price. The reserve country cannot create liquidity in excess of world demand, even if that means accepting slower growth at home. The fire-hose-blast of dollars during the Nixon-Carter years brought the whole system to the brink of collapse. The tenfold runup in oil prices mostly reflected OPEC's implicit switch from the dollar to gold as its pricing standard; over the same period, the dollar also lost half its value against the German mark. Finance ministries were enraged as the value of their dollar reserves plummeted, but no other country had the economic heft to step into America's shoes. When Paul Volcker finally restored monetary order, the dollar soared and the world gratefully settled back into the old system.

Losing Control

The standard fever chart of a country's financial position vis-à-vis the rest of the world is its current account, a kind of international profit and loss statement. Although the current account captures all international spending flows, like tourist spending and earnings from overseas companies, the numbers are dominated by exports and imports. American exports, or everything we sell overseas, go on the plus side of the ledger, while the goods and services we buy from abroad are entered on the minus side.

For about seventy-five years starting in the mid-1890s, the American current account was always strongly in the black. Even during the 1970s oil crisis, the deficit never exceeded $15 billion. The strong flow of earnings from overseas assets, like the European businesses America snapped up in de Gaulle's day, usually offset about half of the oil bill.

The trade account deteriorated steadily through the 1980s and 1990s, before suddenly tilting into free fall about 1999. The 2006 trade deficit was over $750 billion, and the total current account deficit topped $800 billion. The accumulated deficit for 2000 to 2006 is about $4 trillion. Under pressure from the falling dollar, trade numbers improved in the second half of 2007, but the full-year deficit will still be a humongous $650 billion or so. The biggest outflow items in 2006 were oil products at about $300 billion, vehicles at $123 billion, electrical and electronic equipment at $83 billion, and some $200 billion in a grab bag of consumer categories. The biggest item on the plus side was $49 billion in air- and space-related exports.

The $800 billion net outflow in 2006 was more than 6 percent of American GDP. Where did that money come from? Not from consumer savings, for there basically aren't any—household savings have been hovering around zero for the past several years. Nor could it come from public sector savings: Since 2001, the federal government has been about $2 trillion in the red. American companies are sitting on lots of cash, but American investment managers, on net, have sent more than $1 trillion abroad over the past few years.

The answer, of course, is that our deficits are being financed by foreigners—in 2006, the American current account deficit consumed about 70 percent of the rest of the world's surpluses. Most of it comes from private investors—although "private investors" from Russia, China, and the Gulf countries are frequently government fronts—but an increasing amount comes from official sources, mostly central banks. That is a big change. In 2000 and 2001, official sources supplied only about $35 billion a year, but by 2006, the official sources line had ballooned to $440 billion. Much of that, it is safe to assume, are investments made for policy reasons, not because short-term U.S. Treasuries offer unbeatable returns—and policy decisions can be reversed.

The current account presents the net results of a single year's transactions. But if you add up the balance of flows over time, you get a country's net international investment position. At the end of 2006, America's net investment position showed a balance of $2.5 trillion in favor of foreigners. That's a big number.*

Most of those claims are not much to worry about. Americans were upset when the Japanese bought Rockefeller Center in the 1980s, but they couldn't take it back to Japan. The

---

*It is also an understatement. Since 2000, when the investment accounts were roughly in balance, America's $4 trillion in current account deficits should have worsened the net investment position by about that amount. The discrepancy comes from currency-based write-ups of American-owned assets overseas. As the dollar falls against the euro, euro-based assets become worth more in dollar terms, which has improved our net book position by about $1.2 trillion. But those are paper profits, much of it on illiquid bricks-and-mortar assets. The $4 trillion outflow was real money.

growing network of Honda and Toyota factories also go on the deficit side of the ledger, but America is better off that they're here. What is of concern is the large concentrations of cashlike dollar assets held either directly by central banks or other government-controlled bodies. And they are very concentrated. China has $1.2 trillion, as does the rest of non-Chinese Asia. The accumulations in the OPEC nations are perhaps $600 billion. Russia has about $400 billion, and even traditional debtor countries like Mexico and Brazil have large dollar balances. Total foreign-held dollar reserves as of the end of 2006 were somewhere in the neighborhood of $5 trillion.

Should we worry about this? For several years, some very smart people have been arguing that there was little cause for concern, for the current dispensation could be maintained indefinitely. But the rapid fall of the dollar in the last half of 2007 suggests that such hopes were wishful thinking.

The Brief Reign of Bretton Woods II

Ben Bernanke created a minor academic industry with a 2005 lecture that suggested that the persistent, and growing, current account deficit of the United States was not the result of feckless American borrow-and-spend consumption habits, but rather a natural consequence of a "global savings glut."*

---

*There are multiple versions of the story line, which I have conflated into the headline account here, eliding technical differences between "Bretton Woods II," "savings glut," and other theories. But they all conclude that the situation as of, say, 2006 was both natural and stable. Bernanke was not the first to make the argument, but because of his stature, his speech ignited an intense academic and policy debate.

The headline argument went like this. A big emerging country like China had no choice but to adopt an export-led growth strategy, for it lacks the basic banking and credit infrastructure required for an internal consumption-led boom. During the long transition to modernity, it would need to keep industrial wages low to dampen inflation and to moderate the internal stampede to industrial cities. Over time, the buildup of export earnings would provide the capital base for its own modern banking system, while also protecting against the kind of currency and bank runs that hit East Asia in 1997 and 1998. In the meantime, its dollar investments would benefit from the world's deepest, most liquid security and trading markets. The upshot was that for the foreseeable future China, India, the smaller Asian tigers, and the oil exporters would *have to* absorb dollars. Even if the dollar fell steeply, the broader development gains would be worth it.

Although such a state of affairs obviously couldn't last forever, the theory held that it was likely to last a long time—ten to twenty years in most formulations. Natural market forces, in short, would coalesce to create a stable, integrated system of trade and investment flows, with the United States and the dollar at its center. Viewed from a very high altitude, indeed, that would look a lot like the Bretton Woods system that the industrial countries cobbled together after World War II— hence the label Bretton Woods II (hereafter BW2).

Skeptics pointed to worrisome differences. Under the first Bretton Woods, America had all the world's money, so the periphery countries needed to sign up in order to borrow. Under BW2, the center country is still America, but it is now the world's biggest borrower and has a weak currency, while it is the periphery countries that have all the money. Not to worry, the theory went: Today's periphery *needs* to lend to America as badly as the periphery of a half century ago needed to borrow.

One of the subtler attractions of BW2 was how it let policymakers off the hook. Everything is the result of market forces shaping events toward a high-efficiency outcome. The Fed's free-money policy was predetermined by the tidal wave of foreign savings. Alan Greenspan was an agent, not an independent actor. America's housing and debt binge was made in China, and for large and good purposes. Voltaire's Dr. Pangloss knew that if he thought long and hard about the catastrophic Lisbon earthquake, he would see that it was all part of God's benevolent plan.

But as of late 2007, the relentless fall in the value of the dollar was playing havoc with such optimistic assumptions. Since late 2002, when the dollar was roughly at parity with the euro, it has fallen to the point where it takes $1.47 to buy one euro.* Over that same period the dollar price of a British pound has risen from $1.56 to $2.08, while the Brazilian real doubled its value against the dollar. The Canadian dollar was worth only 64 cents in American money in 2002; now it's worth $1.05. The *Economist* has called the dollar's fall the "biggest default in history," exceeding those of any emerging market catastrophe. Many analysts believe that the dollar's

---

*After the euro was rolled out in 1999, it quickly dropped to the point where it cost about 1.20 euros to buy a dollar, which prompted much American chest-thumping about the superiority of the American system. All the comparisons here are November to November.

fall against the euro has been overdone and that it is due for a modest rebound. But the dollar is probably still considerably overvalued against the BRIC countries—Brazil, Russia, India, and China—and on a trade-weighted basis may have substantial further declines in store.

On closer examination, the central premise of the BW2 hypothesis, that large foreign dollar-holders have no choice in the matter, is simply not true; indeed, holding dollars is increasingly against their interests. Start with Russia and the top OPEC exporters. All of these countries price their oil trade in dollars and have been investing their surpluses primarily in dollar-denominated assets. But their primary trade flows are *not* with the United States. Russia, uniquely, trades almost exclusively with Europe and has been taking huge capital and income losses on its dollar balances, while the primary markets for the Middle Eastern oil producers, both for exports and imports, are in Asia.

Asia, indeed, is the linchpin of the BW2 hypothesis. Except for Japan, Asian countries are dollar-based, and the conventional wisdom is that they must stay that way because their economies are tied to China's, and China's trade is primarily with America. The conventional wisdom, in this case, happens to be wrong. China has been working hard to diversify its customer base, and about half of its exports now go to countries outside the United States, Europe, or Japan; mostly they go to other Asian countries, but also to the Middle East and Latin America. America's share of Chinese exports has fallen to just above 20 percent, and Europe recently moved past America on China's customer list. Since almost all Asian countries are becoming large importers of oil and gas, maintaining the implicit dollar peg makes little sense.

Although China has generally good relations with the United States, it is also acutely aware that America is the only important counterweight to Chinese sway over the western Pacific. A gradual Chinese-led Asian currency diversification that weakens the United States not only makes economic sense but also seems very much in its long-term geopolitical interests.

As foreigners tire of absorbing American savings shortfalls, we will have to keep interest rates higher than we would like in order to avert an utter currency rout. With America heading into recession, that is a bitter pill. A continued collapse in the dollar, on the other hand, will inevitably trigger price increases in imported goods, much as it is doing in oil. In short, we are in a box with no good way out. And aside from another quarter-point rate cut or two, there is not much the Fed can do about it.

Events, in any case, are making the BW2 debate academic. The move away from the dollar was already under way by 2006, in almost all surplus countries, and appears to be gathering speed.

Deploying the Surpluses

There are two primary realities about the surpluses of both the oil exporters and of the emerging market countries of Asia. The first is their size, and the second is that they are generally at the disposition of the national governments, or the sovereign. If Great Britain runs a hefty current account surplus, economists might speculate about its impact on local interest rates or the value of the pound, but the question of what Great Britain might *do* with its surplus isn't very meaningful, for it accrues to multiple private parties who will do with it what they wish.

But when trillions of dollars in free cash are at the disposal of governments, the question of what they might do with the money is of prime importance—especially when many of those governments are in various degrees antidemocratic, repressive, or corrupt, often with shadowy ties to criminal or terrorist organizations inimical to the United States. As one might expect, such governments are notoriously close-mouthed about their bank balances and spending habits, leaving it to Western analysts to ferret out the numbers as best they can.

The U.S. Treasury estimated in 2007 that total accumulated surpluses, in all reserve currencies, within the control of sovereigns had risen to $7.6 trillion—that's about 15 percent of global GDP, or more than 60 percent of global savings. Analysts estimate that the oil producers control between a quarter and a third of that, with a median estimate in the range of $2.2 trillion, and East Asia (excluding India and Japan) about the same amount. Japan has about $1 trillion, almost all of it in dollars. Sixty percent of the oil exporter surpluses are owned by just three countries, while twelve countries own essentially all of it. Other than Norway, which is the second-largest surplus country, none of the other major oil states—Russia, the Middle Eastern producers, and Venezuela and Nigeria—is a Western-style democracy. About half of the East Asian surpluses are controlled by China.

Oil prices started shooting up toward the end of 2002, rising steadily from about $30 per barrel to nearly $100 per barrel in late 2007. At least into 2006, however, analysts were relieved to see the oil states continue to invest their windfalls primarily in short-term U.S. Treasuries. They were recycling the petrodollars, just as American banks did in the 1970s and 1980s, except this time back in the direction of America—yet another demonstration of BW2 in action.

In retrospect, the 2003–05 investment pattern may have been just the most expedient way of dealing with such a huge surge of income, for the pattern has clearly changed. Russia was one of the first movers. Its purchases of U.S. dollar assets tracked closely to its accumulating surpluses until the last half of 2006 when, amid sharply rising surpluses, they dropped essentially to zero.

Kuwait, among the closest of America's allies and the third-largest of the Gulf oil producers, dropped its currency's tie to the dollar in May 2007, announcing that it would return to a system of pegging against a basket of reserve currencies. The United Arab Emirates, which includes Abu Dhabi, Dubai, and five other states, seems likely to follow its lead. Initial expectations were that the dollar would make up 75 percent to 80 percent of the Kuwaiti basket, but that is likely to fall as the dollar continues to depreciate. Saudi Arabia is maintaining its fealty to the dollar in public but is quietly distancing itself in fact. By the end of 2006, more than a fifth of its official assets were in nondollar denominations, and it pointedly declined to follow the Federal Reserve's interest-rate reductions in September 2007, although it did follow the Fed's October cut. (Maintaining a currency peg normally requires a country to match interest rate adjustments in the target currency.) Then there are the openly hostile regimes in Iran and Venezuela, which are aggressively whittling down their remaining dollar holdings.

The oil exporters, regardless of their attitudes toward America, really have no choice but to move away from the dollar. With 40 percent of oil-state imports coming from Europe, dollar overweighting makes no sense. Runaway domestic inflation was a big factor in the crash of the oil economies in the 1980s. And the inflation pressures, especially in the Gulf, are intensifying yet again as the falling dollar pushes up the price of nondollar goods, but this time, the sheiks seem determined not to repeat their 1980s mistakes.

China is a different case, since its imports are primarily from East Asia and Japan. But it is acutely conscious of its growing power. China purchased some 55 percent of new U.S. Treasury bond and note issues in 2006, and Federal Reserve models suggest that those purchases by themselves lowered the ten-year rate about 1.5 percent. In response to protectionist demands in the U.S. Congress for a revalued yuan* in the summer of 2007, Chinese officials spoke point-

---

*The Congressional assumption is that a stronger yuan will slow American imports from China and increase exports to China. Any such effect, however, is likely to be small. If Chinese imports became too expensive, most would be replaced by imports from other parts of the world with lower prices. And the class of goods America exports to China—predominantly high-tech capital goods—are not likely to be much influenced by exchange rates. It's also worth noting that the "China effect" on interest rates does *not* support the BW2 story that the credit binge was made in China. The Fed and Treasury were well aware of the incoming investment flows and made a choice to maintain American rates in negative territory.

edly of their "nuclear option." An academic, clearly speaking with official authorization, said:

> China has accumulated a large sum of U.S. dollars. Such a big sum, of which a considerable portion is in U.S. Treasury bonds, contributes a great deal to maintaining the position of the dollar as a reserve currency. Russia, Switzerland, and several other countries have reduced their dollar holdings. China is unlikely to follow suit as long as the yuan's exchange rate is stable against the dollar. The Chinese central bank will be forced to sell dollars once the yuan appreciated dramatically, which might lead to a mass depreciation of the dollar.

In fact, the Chinese have already begun the diversification process, but they are doing it quietly, outside of the official reserve accounts. In that respect, however, they are merely following in the footsteps of almost all the other surplus countries.

The Rise of Sovereign Wealth Funds

The currency crashes in East Asia and Russia in 1997 and 1998 were caused by the practice of borrowing short-term funds in the West and investing them in long-term projects at home. When fears rose that some countries were overextended, Westerners refused to roll over the loans, precipitating a firestorm of local currency crashes and the Russian debt repudiation. Russia and all the Asian countries, including China, which had avoided a currency crash, vowed never again to be at Western mercy. That is the reason they maintain such enormous currency reserves.

But even by the most rigorous standards of banking overseers, the surplus countries as a group now have nearly twice the reserves that could possibly be required for stability insurance. And there's no indication that the hypergrowth of their cash mountain is slowing. Oil surpluses are expected to jump from $750 billion in 2007 to $1 trillion in 2008, especially as Asian demand continues to soar.

The solution is the sovereign wealth fund, or SWF. An SWF is a private investment fund under the broad control of a government but almost always outside of the official finance apparatus, free of the investment limitations that apply to official reserves. The granddaddy of SWFs is Singapore's Temasek Holdings, a $100 billion fund created more than thirty years ago to invest the state's excess reserves. Temasek started reporting publicly in 2004; it claims an 18 percent annual return since inception, and its bonds have a triple-A rating.

At least twenty-five surplus countries already have SWFs or are in the process of setting them up. Their investable funds are now estimated at $3 trillion. Stephen Jen, Morgan Stanley's chief currency economist, points out that even at fairly modest growth rates the holdings of SWFs will exceed all the world's official reserves within about five years.

The Kuwait SWF may be a prototype for a new generation of funds. It is much less secretive than most SWFs and has a capital base of more than $200 billion, or about the same size as America's biggest investor, CALPERS, the California public pension fund. Its manager, Badr Al-Sa'ad, is Western-trained and is consciously mirroring the investment strategies of high-performing endowment funds, like those at Harvard and Yale. He is aggressively shifting the Kuwaiti portfolio from its nearly exclusive focus on U.S. Treasuries to a much greater weighting in equities, with an emphasis on high-growth countries in Asia and on the European fringe, like Turkey. The investment standards Al-Sa'ad uses to measure performance are the Morgan Stanley international indices, suggesting a wide distribution of investments.

The SWFs of Dubai, Abu Dhabi, and Qatar are also quite active, with deals being announced almost weekly. Dubai, in particular, behaves much like an American private equity fund. Recent transactions include a buyout of Tussaud's, the British entertainment group, and a substantial investment in DaimlerChrysler, both of which were later "flipped" at a high profit; Dubai now also has a large stake in Sony. All of the Arab funds like financial markets. Dubai won out over Qatar for a takeover of the Norse-Baltic stock exchange, the OMX, then purchased a substantial stake in the NASDAQ, and as of late November 2007 was facilitating a merger of NASDAQ and OMX, while acquiring NASDAQ's stake in the London Stock Exchange. Other recent Dubai acquisitions include a German aluminum company and a Singapore shipbuilder. Qatar has stakes in the British banks HSBC and Standard Chartered and in European Airbus, while Abu Dhabi has purchased a large stake in the American chip-builder AMD and, of course, now has a nearly 5 percent position in Citigroup. A Saudi prince has for many years been a 3 percent shareholder in Citi.

Russia is in the process of dividing its excess reserves into an oil stabilization fund and a savings fund. The stabilization fund receives all oil revenues above $27 per barrel and will top out at 10 percent of GDP. It is intended to stabilize internal finances in the event of a fall in oil prices and is conservatively invested in high-quality debt instruments, with a 45–55 U.S./European split. Its savings fund will presumably follow Russia's current pattern of opportunistic equity investments, primarily in energy properties. European countries, however, have recently blocked several Russian acquisitions, fearing their increasing dependence on Russian oil and natural gas.

China has long been making infrastructure and energy investments throughout Latin American and Africa, especially in Nigeria, one of the most important American energy suppliers. China also recently partnered with the Singapore SWF in a failed attempt to take a large position in Barclays bank.

Finally, Japan, from America's perspective, the most reliable large holder of dollar assets, is believed to be investing its huge dollar reserves mostly in U.S. Treasuries. While Japan justifies its large accumulations as a hedge against its looming pension expenses, its funds management is coming under internal criticism for not maximizing returns. Pressure is building for much greater diversification and for SWF-type strategies.

The scramble for SWF cash from American private equity and hedge funds borders on the unseemly. China has purchased a stake in the Blackstone Group, and Chinese funds are reportedly in negotiation with three other American private equity firms. One of them is apparently the Carlyle Group, which has long been a high-priced retirement home for former top government executives, including notables like George H. W. Bush, James Baker, and former British Prime Minister John Major. Carlyle also sold a $1.35 billion stake to

Abu Dhabi, while Dubai took a $1.15 billion position in the Ochs-Ziff hedge fund. For SWFs, well-connected private equity and hedge funds offer ideal political coverage for a drive to increase ownership of American and European assets. The fund managers think of themselves as supranational—they just follow the money.

From one angle, none of this is inconsistent with BW2: You just have to follow the symmetries with Bretton Woods I, all the way through. De Gaulle's complaint with BW1, recall, was that the dollar seigniorage became an engine for America's buying up foreign assets on the cheap. Precisely the same thing is now happening under BW2. But just as in BW1, the seigniorage accrues to the funding countries—in effect, the lords of the manor are Arab, Russian, and Chinese, while the peasant maidens are American. De Gaulle would have been delighted.

It won't be an easy adjustment for the United States. Two quite plausible foreign acquisitions, in 2005 and 2006, were sidetracked by Congressional howls over their national security implications. The 2005 dustup was triggered by a Chinese state oil company's bid for Unocal, which had been put into play by other bidders. As only the twelfth-largest American oil company, Unocal was hardly a strategic asset, and its properties were primarily on the Chinese periphery—just the kind of rationalizing acquisition that investment banks promote all the time. The Chinese were shocked at the American reaction. The second deal involved Dubai's purchase of a controlling stock interest in a London global port operator, who also happened to run a large swathe of American ports. Dubai, one of America's closest Gulf allies, thought it was making a portfolio investment. It didn't have any management role and certainly wasn't "Arabizing" operations. The purchase went through, but the London company was forced to sell its American operations, almost certainly at a discount.

But we'd better get used to it. Analysts have calculated that the creation of the Chinese SWF by itself will raise American interest rates by 1/2 percent, just by the implied diversion of funds that previously flowed into Treasuries. Over the past decade, America has made itself a savings-poor country and will be running financial deficits with the rest of the world for the foreseeable future.

There are only two paths to raising the savings we need to invest and grow. The first is to make deep and wrenching changes in the way Americans use their money. The second is to attract some of it back from abroad. As a practical matter, we will have to do both. But the days when foreigners were willing to finance our deficits for free are gone forever; now we will be selling the family jewels. IBM, anyone? Its 2007 market value is only about $160 billion. Saudi Arabia could swallow that in a single gulp.

All in all, it's hard to imagine a worse outcome—the United States, the "hyperpower," the global leader in the efficiency of its markets and the productivity of its businesses and workers, hopelessly in hock to some of the world's most unsavory regimes. But that's where a quarter-century of diligent sacrifice to the gods of the free market has brought us. It's a disgrace.

CHAPTER 5 POSTSCRIPT

In the first edition of this book, this chapter ended with the paragraph:

> The recent woes of the dollar are important for our story because they effectively take the Fed off the board. As the credit crunch works its way through banks and investment banks over the next year or so, there will be no soothing fountains of new dollars coming out of Washington. The days of a universal put to the Federal Reserve are finally over.

I could not have been more wrong. Ben Bernanke, in close cooperation with Treasury Secretary Hank Paulson, embarked on round after round of creative intervention unmatched in the entire history of the Fed. His activities have received relatively little attention amid the clamor over the U.S. Treasury's $700 billion "TARP" (Troubled Asset Rescue Program) law, the crisis on Wall Street, and the evolving collapse of the global banking system. But if the creativity of the Bernanke/Paulson interventions has been unparalleled, so arguably are the risks to America's economic future if they fail.

My mistake was to assume that Bernanke would be limited to the policy arsenal the Fed had used for the previous seventy years—which basically comes down to managing the Fed Funds rate. In late 2007, when the first edition of this book went to press, Fed Funds were at 4.25 percent. And with the dollar sliding rapidly against the euro and oil prices ticking up,

Bernanke seemed to have little scope for further reductions. In fact, he cut rates very aggressively, all the way down to 1 percent in October—although the rate cuts turned out to be just a minor sidelight in his new bag of tricks. But to understand his new tools, we need a short primer on the workings of the Federal Reserve.

The Fed, to begin with, is a bank. Like other banks, its assets are its loans and investments, which it finances by incurring liabilities, like debt and deposits from member banks. In the normal case, almost all of the Fed's assets are loans to the government, in the form of Treasury bills, notes, and bonds; while its primary liabilities are its own debt certificates. Everyone is familiar with Fed debt certificates; they carry the legend "Federal Reserve Note," are colored green, and we use them as money.

The economic role of the Fed is to stabilize the supply of money so it is neither too plentiful, which can generate inflation, nor too scarce. If it issues more currency to buy Treasuries from its member banks, they should become more liquid and more willing to lend, thus stimulating economic activity, and vice versa.

Bernanke, however, is also a serious academic who has devoted much of his career to analyzing central bank behavior during the Great Depression. He is the lead author of a 2004 Federal Reserve working paper exploring the Fed's policy alternatives "At the Zero Bound," or the point where the usual tools of interest rate policy cease to have any effect on the real economy.

In the paper, Bernanke poses a common policy conundrum. It sometimes happens that pushing down Fed Funds rates has no impact on medium- or long-term rates, which may be a more important determinant of business lending. Indeed, if markets are worried about inflation, adding liquidity could even cause a *rise* in longer term rates.

In such a case, Bernanke suggests, the Fed could "change the composition of its balance sheet," by preferentially acquiring specific types of assets. "If the Federal Reserve were willing to purchase an unlimited amount of a particular asset, say, a Treasury security, at a fixed price, there is little doubt that it could establish that asset's price," Bernanke writes. But he also warns that the Fed should be "cautious" about such a strategy, since its actual effects would be "quite uncertain."

Starting in late 2007, and continuing ever more aggressively through 2008, Bernanke started precisely such an experiment in using the Fed's purchasing power to target asset prices. But instead of targeting specific maturities of Treasuries, he targeted the illiquid assets weighing down bank balance sheets. In effect, he was conducting a live experiment to see if the Fed could establish a floor-price for the CDOs and other complex paper that were being violently written down by bank accountants.

The first attempt, in December 2007, was appropriately cautious—it was relatively small and short-term, was open only to Federal Reserve system member banks, and was circumspect on acceptable securities. But step-by-step, Bernanke expanded the eligible borrowers—from Federal Reserve member banks to broker-dealers; then to AIG, an insurance company; and most recently, by lending directly to major corporations seeking to borrow in the unsecured, short-term "commercial paper" market.

At the same time, Bernanke just as steadily increased the volume and the range of targeted securities he would lend against—including even "investment-grade" (translation: "anything not junk"), sub-prime mortgage backed CDOs. (The Fed takes triple-A rated subprime mortgage CDOs at 98 cents on the dollar. Those are the same class of securities that Merrill Lynch sold for 22 cents on the dollar just before its merger with Bank of America.)

The Fed's weekly balance sheet is a fever-chart of Bernanke's interventions. Start with the balance sheet of October 2007, when the Fed was still operating in a more or less normal mode. Total Fed assets were $890 billion, of which $780 billion comprised Treasuries, with the balance scattered among gold certificates, physical plant, and other miscellany—all roughly of the size, and in the proportions, as they had been for several years.

Now jump ahead to the balance sheet from October 29, 2008. The Fed's assets had swelled to $2 *trillion*, an increase of 125 percent. But only $269 billion were in Treasuries actually held at the Fed. The rest were a mélange of god-knows-what instruments vacuumed up from banks and investment banks. There were $301 billion of risky securities exchanged for Treasuries in bi-weekly auctions. There was $370 billion in "Other Loans"; we know little about them except that they include the credit extension to AIG, which had climbed to $123 billion. There was a special $27 billion line for Bear Stearns; $145 billion in the corporate commercial paper program; and $540 billion in "Other Assets." Those seem to be dollars swapped out to foreign central banks, to help them fund local banks who need dollars to deleverage their dollar-based CDOs and other poison apples bought from America.

The total lending expansion, therefore, was about $1.1 trillion. It all happened in about ten weeks, starting in mid-September, just as Congress was debating the TARP bill to purchase banks' bad assets or otherwise provide them with new equity. About $650 billion of the new lending took place during the TARP debate, although it continued at only a slightly slower pace through October.

In other words, even as academics and Congress agonized over TARP, Bernanke, with the active assistance of Treasury Secretary Hank Paulson, pumped out roughly the same amount of money, without so much as asking a by-your-leave. Paulson even engineered a special $400 billion Treasury borrowing program—i.e., increased the federal debt—to supply part of the extra cash needed to support Bernanke's lending.

In principle, of course, the Fed could hold soybeans on its balance sheet—Treasuries have no more intrinsic value than the Fed's notes. But the radical shift in balance-sheet quality makes overseas investors nervous. If the Fed balance sheet starts to look like those of the banks it's bailing out, it could readily shake confidence in America's economic soundness.

A more substantive reason for nervousness is that the Fed balance sheet is the foundation stone for the American money supply. The "Monetary Base," or "high-powered money," is the sum of outstanding Federal Reserve notes—the circulating currency—plus free bank reserves on deposit at the Fed. Under normal conditions, the Monetary Base and the Fed's balance sheet are approximately the same number, since the one is more or less the flip side of the other. A radical expansion of the Fed balance sheet raises fears that America may attempting to simply inflate its way out of its problems, much as it tried to do—so disastrously—in the 1970s.

When Bernanke first started his asset purchase program, however, he was careful not to issue additional currency. Instead, he exchanged Treasuries for the securities he was taking from the banks. He could argue, therefore, that he was merely changing the composition of the Fed's balance sheet, not its size, so the money supply would not be affected. But that is disingenuous at best. Money supply is the product of the stock of money—the Monetary Base—times the velocity with which it turns over. By replacing illiquid CDOs and such with highly leverageable Treasuries, he was increasing velocity, and revving up banks' ability to supply credit. Increasing the money supply was the whole point of the exercise.

The Fed also contended that the massive expansion of the Fed's balance sheet in September and October would have minimal impact on the money supply. The $145 billion in commercial paper surely does, of course, for it is clearly pushing out new cash for paper. But Paulson's special issue of $400 billion in Treasuries, rather than new issuances of greenbacks, financed most of the rest. Since Paulson's sale of Treasuries soaked up an equivalent amount of currency, the argument goes, the total money supply should be unaffected. But that may depend on where it was placed; if foreign governments bought the treasuries from their offshore troves of dollars, which is likely, the new lending in America still might have an inflationary effect.

The truth is, no one knows or ever will, for even in retrospect it will be impossible to untangle cause-and-effect relations. But if we have learned anything from the frenzied interventions of

the past year, it is the power of the law of unintended consequences. Interestingly, at the height of Bernanke's interventions,
there was a general *tightening* of lending conditions. Some market watchers worried that interbank liquidity was drying up
precisely because borrowing at the Fed was so much easier. Only
time will tell.

The larger question may be: Are there any limits to the policies we will undertake to stave off the dreaded "Recession"—
which seems now to be viewed as a disaster on the scale of the
1960s specter of nuclear Armageddon? But we have to have a
recession. The prosperity of the 2000s was fake, based on massive consumer borrowing on bubble-priced assets. Now consumers are deeply in debt, and the price of the favored assets
are falling, while both employment and incomes are falling
along with them. Pouring out ever more dollars in the hope of
recovering the zing of the old bubble days is exactly the wrong
prescription, and risks making eventual outcomes far worse
than they need to be.

CHAPTER 6

The Great Unwinding

In Chapter 4 we saw how lenders or companies who want to get risky assets off their books could package and sell them as collateralized debt obligations, or CDOs. Suppose you own a portfolio of high-yield bonds with a below-investment-grade rating. To construct the CDO, you put the portfolio into a trust and create a family of bonds with different claims to the portfolio's cash flows. The top-tier bonds, which might be 80 percent of the total, get first dibs on *all* cash flows. Since those bonds are almost certain to be fully paid, they get a top credit rating, and conservative investors, like pension funds, are happy to take them off your hands. The rest of the bonds are queued up in the payments "waterfall," with each successive layer bearing greater risk, paying higher yields, and getting lower ratings.

We also saw how credit default swaps could be used to create synthetic CDOs. A credit default swap allows the holder of a risky asset to lay off the risk to a third party, without having to sell the asset. With imagination, some advanced math, and some computer wizardry, a family of credit default swaps can be constructed that will generate exactly the same risks and cash flows as some real reference CDO portfolio, but without the trouble of actually assembling the loans—a synthetic CDO. The growth of synthetics means that the actual supply of real subprime mortgages or highly leveraged corporate loans is no longer a limit on creating CDOs based on those instruments. There is also a tendency for synthetic CDOs to distribute only the riskiest, highest-yielding layers to outside investors, so they may increase the proportion of high-risk paper in the market.

But we ended Chapter 4 with a question. The limiting factor in creating CDOs is finding buyers for the bottom tranche—the equity tranche, or toxic waste—that absorbs the first dollar losses from an entire portfolio. The enormous scale of the CDO industry suggests that somebody's been buying a lot of toxic waste. Who is it?

Well, they must be investors willing to take on tremendous risk to earn superior returns. And they must have considerable freedom to invest as they choose. Ideally, they wouldn't have to disclose the details of their positions to nervous shareholders or trustees. They would need access to huge amounts of investable funds and must be free to leverage up their positions to enhance returns. Yes, as the reader has already guessed, it's the hedge funds. And the entire industry is dancing to their tune.

Hedge Funds, Credit Derivatives, and CDOs

Hedge funds* are unregulated investment vehicles that cater to institutions and wealthy individuals, and promise extraordinary returns. There are few limits on how they invest, what kind of risks they take, and how much leverage they use. The top performers truly have achieved spectacular results, some over very long periods. But as the field has gotten ever more crowded, average returns have been decidedly lackluster, especially given the industry's outsized pay packages. As of mid-2007, hedge funds deployed an estimated $2 trillion to $2.5 trillion of equity capital, and much higher economic capital due to their aggressive use of leverage.

A large subsegment of hedge funds now concentrate in CDOs and credit default swaps. They account for about 60 percent of all trading in credit default swaps—that's a $45 trillion market—and for about a third of CDO trading. All the evidence is that they are especially concentrated in the riskiest classes of credit-related products. There are other redoubts of CDO equity buyers: It is a favored alternative investment for life insurance companies and for some Asian banks looking for high returns to offset their high funding

---

*The term "hedge fund" dates from the 1950s when a new class of investment funds adopted long-short stock trading strategies. You'd buy, or go long, a steel company stock you liked but hedge the risk by shorting, or betting against, another steel stock you thought was weaker. If all steel stocks fell for some reason, the profits on the short position would offset the loss on your long position. Long-short is still a common hedge fund strategy, but by no means the dominant one.

costs. But they are not leveraged like hedge funds and are not usually active traders.

What is the attraction of the market for hedge funds? Let's assume I am a pension fund manager with a risky $10 million subprime mortgage portfolio that I'd like to get off my books. I could try to sell it, but it would be quicker and easier to enter into a $10 million credit default swap on a suitable tranche of the ABX, a widely used index of subprime CDOs. In mid-October 2007 a midcredit "A" swap on the ABX was trading at about 60, down from a par of 100. That discount means that the market expected the all-in cost of defaults in this tranche of the index CDOs to be 40 cents on the dollar in today's money. The counterparty to my swap—it's probably a hedge fund—guarantees that I'll get $10 million back at the end of the index term, which is standardized at five years. What does it cost me? Since the index is at 60, I pay the counterparty $4 million up front to cover the risk he's assuming. (I'll also pay him interest at a standardized rate, but that should be covered by the interest I'm collecting on my own mortgages.) The result is that I've crystallized my worries into a single payment, taken the hit, and no longer have subprime exposure.*

---

*Note that I've assumed that my portfolio will behave approximately the same as the ABX reference list of twenty deals. Each of those deals is a CDO of at least $500 million, containing thousands of mortgages, so they are a good market sample. The ABX is tranched into five risk classes, so I could pick whichever one was the best match. Until recently, the vast majority of credit default swaps were individually tailored, but the advent of the indexes, which are quite liquid, reduces the expense of one-off hedging. The upfront payment applies only when the swap is trading below par. If it is above par, as many ABX swaps were not long ago, the upfront payment goes in the other direction.

And what does the hedge fund that sold the protection get out of the deal? It gets *cash*. Cash that could be booked as income—and fund partners typically get 20 percent of all income—and cash that could be leveraged up into bigger and bigger deals. Yes, that upfront payment came with a liability, but hedge funds are experts at understating future liabilities. Since so many hedge funds have not been living up to their performance promises, the riskiest segments of the structured credit netherworld will look very attractive.

Fitch, the credit rating agency, made a survey of credit-related hedge funds' trading practices at the end of 2006. Their informants were the hedge fund prime brokers—the banks that perform hedge funds' day-to-day brokerage, clearing, and other trading functions, and finance their trading positions. A handful of the very biggest banks dominate hedge fund prime brokerage, with Morgan Stanley, Goldman, J. P. Morgan Chase, and Deutschebank topping most lists. Reportedly, the prime broker banks get up to 20 percent to 30 percent of their total bank revenues from hedge funds, including underwriting and deal fees. So hedge funds are *very* important customers.

Here's what the prime brokers told Fitch.

The hedge funds' appetite for the riskiest positions has made them a major source of liquidity in the CDO and credit default swap markets. Their willingness to employ leverage to maximize those positions amplifies their impact. The funds' persistent demand for higher-yield products is pushing the industry up the risk ladder into CDOs constructed from second-lien loans, bridge financings, private equity, and other less liquid assets, often with minimal protections for higher-tier buyers.

Hedge funds consistently pressure prime brokers for more leverage and easier credit so they can keep expanding positions. They are demanding, and frequently getting, locked-in funding levels for terms of up to 180 days, which limits prime broker control over the riskiness of their positions. Although prime brokers are supposed to monitor their clients' overall balance sheets and total margining, they concede that they typically do not have access to that information. The shift in credit hedge fund investing away from cash-flow CDOs toward credit derivatives, Fitch reports, "introduces its own unique risks that have not been fully tested in a credit downturn . . . [and] could foster greater short-term price instability."

Fitch concludes the survey by lamenting the "instability of hedge funds as an investor class," because of their reliance on short-term, margin-based lending. Since the funds do not have direct relationships with the borrowers in CDO portfolios, Fitch worries as well that they would have no incentive to cooperate in borrower workouts during an unwinding episode—another case of the Agency problem.

The common factor underlying all of these concerns is very high leveraging of credit-related hedge funds. Here is the math. Credit-related hedge funds typically leverage their equity five to ten times. Assume a fund is leveraged 5:1—for every dollar of its own capital, it invests four more borrowed from one of its prime broker banks. Now assume it wants to buy the lowest, or equity, tranche of a big CDO. A normal CDO's equity tranche with fairly risky underlying assets might absorb, say, 5 percent of the portfolio's first losses. A hedge fund that buys that position would be leveraged 20:1—since a loss of just 1/20, or 5 percent, of the portfolio wipes out its entire position. Walk through the deal sequence in detail:

- Hedge fund (HF) raises cash by selling equity in the form of partnership shares.
- For every $1 invested from its partnership equity, HF invests $4 more borrowed from its banks, so its equity investments are leveraged 5:1.
- HF buys $100 million in first-loss bonds underpinning a $2 billion CDO. First-loss bonds are therefore leveraged 20:1. The $100 million purchase, however, is financed with $20 million of HF equity and $80 million of bank lending. The bonds are kept in a bank margin account to secure the loan to HF.
- HF partners are therefore leveraged 5 x 20 = 100:1. A loss of 1 percent on the CDO wipes out all HF partner equity.

Now assume the CDO incurs a 3 percent loss.

- The value of the bonds in the margin account is now only $40 million.
- HF has lost its entire $20 million equity investment and half of the bank's $80 million loan. HF must supply an additional $40 million to the margin account, in cash or good securities, to make good the bank's losses.
- HF must supply a further $8 million margin to restore its agreed 5:1 bank leverage ratio. The remaining $40

million bond position, that is, is financed by $32 million in bank borrowings, and $8 million in HF cash equity.

- HF's total equity outlay has now grown to $68 million. An additional 2 percent adverse move, of course, will wipe all that out and will require an additional $32 million repayment to the bank, for a total cash loss of $100 million.

In other words, these are very risky investments that can turn very fast. If this were the only CDO in trouble, our hedge fund would probably have no trouble stumping up the required extra margin. But since CDOs are often representative of an asset type, a raft of similar CDOs is likely to be experiencing similar problems. And now we're into a replay of the June 2007 Bear Stearns subprime hedge funds' liquidity confrontation. The bank demands its cash, the hedge fund pleads straitened circumstances, the bank seizes assets and tries to sell them, and the doors blow off the market.

Hedge funds, moreover, must generally use mark-to-market accounting, as do banks and investment banks in their trading accounts. Mark-to-market means that at regular periods, usually on a daily basis for deeply traded instruments, your portfolio securities must be revalued at their current market price. Value increases are reported as trading profits, and value decreases as trading losses.

Now let's look at mark-to-market accounting for a structured investment, like a CDO. When the subprime CDO market first took off in 2005, subprime mortgage defaults were only in the 3 percent range. A 20 percent cushion of equity and mezzanine debt for the top layer seemed like ample protection, so rating agencies generally assigned triple-A and double-A ratings to the top 80 percent of bonds in the CDO. Residential mortgage CDOs are generally priced off the ten-year swap rate, an interbank funding rate that tracks closely to ten-year Treasuries. During 2005, the swap rate was as low as 4.4 percent, and top CDO tranches were being priced at a spread of only 10 to 25 basis points (hundredths of a percent), i.e., in the range of 4.5 percent to 4.65 percent.

Assume you hold a triple-A rated subprime CDO bond that pays 5 percent. With default rates now trending toward 10 percent and rising, your protection is dissolving fast, and your bond no longer justifies a triple-A rating. Banks and rating agencies have sophisticated models for revising the marks, but a handy proxy might be the yield required to issue new, decent-quality subprime mortgages, which is at least 9.5 percent. (As your protection dissolves, you're basically just holding subprime mortgages.) If an investor wants a ten-year bond or mortgage with a 9.5 percent yield, how much will she pay for one with just a 5 percent coupon? The answer is about 70 cents on the dollar. So if you paid $1 million par value for a 5 percent CDO, you've taken a $300,000 loss. There is a tendency to wave off mark-to-market losses as paper losses. No, they are *real* losses; if you paid $1,000 for something that is worth only $700, you have lost $300.

Something like that is what happened at Bear. Ralph Cioffi, the Bear hedge fund manager, protested that he had bought mostly high-quality double-A- and triple-A-rated CDO bonds and that they were all still performing, in the sense that they hadn't defaulted. But you don't have to default to lose value. 2005- and 2006-vintage CDOs were priced as if they were almost as safe as U.S. Treasuries. They're not. They're fairly risky instruments. But since they carry only Treasury-like yields, their real value is falling and will continue to fall as defaults mount.

There is substantial evidence that credit hedge funds do not accurately mark their holdings. A detailed survey by Deloitte Financial Services suggests that fewer than half of hedge funds consistently follow best-practice asset valuation and portfolio stress-testing practices. In a number of funds, asset valuation was at the sole discretion of fund managers, despite the obvious conflict of interests. Some hedge funds, it appears, also make a practice of trading assets to each other at favorable prices, sometimes with buyback provisions, in order to establish fake mark-to-market pricing. Sloppy or misleading valuations inexorably and invisibly increase true leverage, ensuring bigger blowups.

The Bear incident also nicely illustrates the balance of terror between the banks and their hedge fund clients. Indeed, the banks' grousing in the Fitch report may reflect their unhappiness with that position. In the Bear crisis, Merrill Lynch was the most aggressive of the banks in forcing collateral calls; and just a few months later, partly in consequence of its own aggressiveness, Merrill booked a huge profit hit from the ensuing market meltdown. Banks, that is, are deeply in bed with their hedge fund clients, with massive amounts of money at risk. The temptation not to trigger value hits, and to let unsound positions build, is very strong. But substantial reversals in any important asset class leave no place to hide. Sooner or later, the banks will have no choice but to start seizing assets, even at the risk of opening the gates to un-shirted hell.

To read the newspaper reports, the credit crunch is a sub-prime crisis. It's much broader than that. Subprime may support the largest single class of troubled CDOs, but the credit problems in other sectors are about as large and at least as grave.

The Company Debt Bubble

The junk bonds that Drexel Burnham and Michael Milken first used to finance corporate takeovers, now renamed high-yield bonds, have become a mainstream financing tool for almost any healthy company of any size, and a standard portfolio asset even for retail investors. Since a market shakeout from 1989 to 1991, the overall rate of high-yield issuance has steadily increased, and the credit quality of the bonds has steadily deteriorated. Amazingly, the interest yields demanded by investors have dropped just as steadily as the average quality of the credits.

According to Standard and Poor's, over the past fifteen years the median rating for all bond issuances slipped from a solid investment-grade A- to BBB-, the rating just above junk or speculative-grade bonds. Most of the highly rated companies, moreover, are concentrated in the glamour names of the financial sector. Only 39 percent of nonfinancial issuers now have investment-grade ratings, while issuance of very risky CCC/CC-rated debt has tripled. High-yield bonds, in short, are now the market mainstream.

After the tech bubble popped in 2000, high-yield default rates trended sharply upward, approaching 13 percent in 2002, against a long-term annual average of about 3 percent. As the flood of liquidity from the Federal Reserve took hold, however, default rates plummeted to just 0.76 percent in 2006. It was the lowest rate of defaults since 1981, when the junk bond world as we know it was still a gleam in Drexel's eye. Through the first half of 2007, it was even lower, at just 0.26 percent. Interest spreads on high-yield debt tightened commensurately. New York University's Edward Altman, a leading academic expert on bond yields, has calculated that mid-2007 high-yield rates implied that investors anticipated only a 1 percent annual rate of high-yield defaults and a 50 percent recovery rate. In effect, investors priced in the expectation of balmy markets for the long haul. Leveraged loans, or high-risk paper structured in the form of bank loans, usually in connection with a leveraged buyout, recently have been taking the credit spotlight away from high-yield bonds,* but credit and quality issues are much the same.

What accounts for such low default rates? The Greenspan school of market sages points to the new credit paradigm. Securitization and new credit hedging instruments have dampened market volatility and broadened the availability of credit. In addition, private equity funds often can organize partial

---

*Private equity funds often prefer financing through leveraged loans, since they can be secured by company assets, whereas bonds are generally unsecured. Since leveraged loans are so deeply subordinated, the security isn't worth a lot, but it gives them precedence over pre-existing high-yield bonds in a bankruptcy. The shift to loans, in short, is a way for private equity funds to squeeze out previous debt investors in healthy companies.

liquidations and restructurings much more efficiently than traditional bankruptcy courts, so defaults can be cleaned up much faster than through traditional mechanisms. All those claims are true—up to a point—but they were also true, up to a point, in subprime mortgages.

Leveraged loans resemble subprime mortgages in many other ways as well. Banks or other lenders originate the loans on behalf of private equity funds but quickly pass them on to CLO (collateralized loan obligations) investors. The buyout funds often put up little equity, and deals are usually closed with bank-provided equity bridge financing that gets taken out when the CLO bonds are sold. Hedge funds are major liquidity providers for CLOs, just as they are for CDOs, and total leverage for the equity CLO investors and the private equity fund deal investors is typically in the 100:1 range. Just as in the latter stages of the subprime market, deal terms are being stretched to accommodate ever-more risky borrowers. There has even been a resurrection of PIK, or payment-in-kind, notes—"death spiral" notes not seen since the last frenzied days of the 1989 junk bond blowup. (The notes allow you to pay interest with more notes. Keep missing interest and your debt curve swoops toward infinity.) U.S. takeover leverage ratios—debt service divided by total cash flow—increased by 50 percent from 2002 through the first half of 2007, while cash extractions by private equity owners were quite high.

When the subprime crisis hit in the summer of 2007, the leveraged loan and high-yield market came to a grinding halt, leaving the banks ruefully holding at least $300 billion to $400 billion of buyout bridge-equity lending commitment that they feared they could not lay off to CLO investors. Several prominent deals cratered and several of those went to court. As of late November, the market was still in near-stasis, although smaller deals were getting done. By unhappy coincidence, the $300 billion to $400 billion that banks are potentially on the hook for in takeover loans is almost exactly the same as the potential obligations they face as their structured investment vehicles, or SIVs, continue to unravel. According to the *Financial Times*, in October 2007 several big banks were negotiating discounted lending terms to vulture funds, firms that specialize in distressed debt, on the condition that they use the money to buy the same banks' deal-related leveraged loans. This is a snake fighting starvation by eating its tail.

The corporate sector as a whole, it is frequently pointed out, is not highly leveraged. Profits have been very high during most of the 2000s, and capital spending has been soft, so companies built up big cash balances, although they mostly have been paid out in dividends or in stock buybacks. But of total outstanding corporate debt—$5.7 trillion as of year-end 2006—nearly a third of it is lower-quality. High-yield bond outstandings are about $1.1 trillion, while the total of syndicated leveraged loans and leveraged loans in CLOs, mostly related to takeovers, is at least as high. In the corporate market, much as in the mortgage market, the majority of borrowers are conservatively financed but the leveraged borrowers tend to be *very* leveraged. And as happened with the subprime markets, rising defaults in the highly leveraged categories will raise the costs of credit across the entire asset class.

A comprehensive 2006 survey of private equity practices by the British Financial Services Authority (FSA) drew explicit parallels with the subprime markets. Private-equity companies were "increasingly being financed . . . with a capital structure that is unsustainable in the long term," that is, counting on takeouts by CLOs and CDOs. "[T]he riskiest tranches of leveraged finance debt is concentrated amongst a relatively small community of fund/structured product managers employing leverage." The committee expressly warned that corporate debt markets could create a "financial stability level event," civil service–speak for a credit-market Chernobyl.

It may be worth noting that as the FSA was completing its report, Alan Greenspan was still singing the praises of the new credit technologies for their role in "lay[ing] off all the risk of highly leveraged institutions—and that's what banks are, highly leveraged institutions—on stable American and international institutions." CDOs and credit hedge funds apparently now count as "stable American and international institutions."

And It Keeps Getting Worse

A number of other very large credit sectors are on the brink of extremely difficult times.

Credit Card Debt—This is a $915 billion investor's market, almost all of which is securitized, although usually not in structured instruments like CDOs. Credit card debt has not grown rapidly in recent years, as homeowners opted to finance consumer purchases by borrowing on their houses.

Now that the home equity loan market has all but dried up, credit card debt is rising. Stock markets idiotically reacted gleefully when consumption expenditures held firm in the third quarter of 2007, but much of it was financed by a big jump in credit card revolving debt. That is a path to disaster. The interest charged on card balances for good credit risks approaches 20 percent and can be as high as 40 percent for the less qualified.* Although delinquencies are still low, they have started to rise noticeably, and most big banks are increasing their loan-loss reserves. A housing bubble in Great Britain imploded in early 2006. Since then, according to *Fortune*, credit card charge-offs and delinquencies are up about 50 percent. In a twist, consumers are apparently using credit card debt to make payments on their mortgages, a hopeless strategy. Assuming a substantial recession in the United States, which is increasingly likely, write-offs in the 5 percent to 10 percent range are reasonable guesses.

CMBS (Commercial Mortgage-Backed Securities)—These are CDO-like structures based on commercial mortgages for office buildings, condos, factories, and the like. They have enjoyed a very fast run since 2005, but the market visibly stalled in the third quarter of 2007. Despite very aggressive financings from late 2006 through the first half of 2007, top-rated CMBS tranches were routinely sold at less than 1/10 percent

---

* The subprime credit card industry is often viciously exploitative. A recent wrinkle is cards with no limits and no fees, except a "refundable acceptance fee." If the holder makes a prescribed number of minimum payments *prior* to using the card, the "acceptance fee" is refunded in small increments. Missed payments add interest to the acceptance fee. Poor people sign up for the cards and make a few payments before they realize they're being bilked.

over the swap spreads. There are now a number of prominent properties in which building cash flow will not cover the interest due on the equity CMBS tranches. All CMBS spreads started widening rapidly in fall 2007, leading to substantial mark-to-market losses. Reportedly, CMBS "warehouses" in large banks are accumulating large balances of unsold CMBS rather than risk a large mark-to-market hit from a failed sale. This is an $800 billion market. Bad performance on the poorly underwritten 2006/2007-vintage deals will cause mark-to-market woes across the industry.

Monoline Insurers—These are among the least known and potentially most disruptive of credit sectors. They are mostly publicly traded companies (Ambac and MBIA are among the best known) that write insurance protecting purchasers against principal losses on securities. The business evolved as a kind of credit review service for municipal bonds. Since so many local government entities issue bonds, it is impractical for investors to monitor them on their own. An "insurance wrap" from one of the monolines gradually evolved as a near-standard requirement for new muni issues. For the wrap to be useful, however, the insurers must maintain their triple-A credit ratings.

Over the past few years, however, the monolines have expanded their business into insuring the triple-A-rated tranches of mortgage-backed CDOs. Because municipal bond defaults are so rare, they have traditionally required little capital relative to their insurance liabilities and maintained roughly the same ratios on their CDO insurance business. Collectively, they have written principal and interest insurance on about $3.3 trillion of instruments, on a collective capital base of only $22 billion, which is a leverage ratio of 150:1. Given the turmoil in CDOs, the monolines' triple-A ratings at that level of leverage are absurd. In October 2007, Fitch began a credit review, raising the possibility of a downgrade, and by late November, the market spreads on credit default swaps on Ambac, arguably the industry flagship, had risen to junk-bond levels.

As this book goes to press, the position of the monolines would be comic, if it weren't so serious. Although the market rates Ambac as a junk-caliber company, its name as a backup on a similarly risky CDO bond transmutes the bond into a triple-A credit. The alchemy is possible only because the rating agencies have so far grimly stuck with their triple-A rating of Ambac. But everyone knows that they are maintaining that pretense only out of fear of precipitating a wave of downgrades on another $2 trillion to $3 trillion of bonds. In short, we are stuck in an "Emperor's Wonderful New Clothes" moment. Even as the Treasury, the financial press, and the banks roundly criticize the rating agencies for their wild overratings of CDOs, there is growing alarm at the possibility of a realistic rating of the monolines. Should some innocent point out that the emperor is really naked, chaos may ensue.

Credit Default Swaps—Finally, we get to what is potentially the most catastrophic risk of all. Credit default swaps, as we've seen, are a form of insurance contract. If I own a company or CDO bond, I can protect myself against principal loss by entering into a credit default swap with a counterparty who promises to make good my losses in the event of a default. Portfolios covered by default swap contracts ballooned from about $1 trillion in 2001 to about $45 trillion in mid-2007.

Credit default swaps are not traded on exchanges; they instead are private deals arranged for a fee by broker-dealer banks.

According to a recent analysis in Peter L. Bernstein's respected market letter, *Economic and Portfolio Strategy*, outstanding default swap contracts cover, in roughly equal proportions, company, or "single-name," bond or loan credits, various credit indexes like the ABX, and structured finance instruments, like CDOs and CLOs. The sellers of the protection, or the guarantors, primarily are banks and hedge funds. Banks are on the hook to make good losses on some $18.2 trillion of portfolios, while credit hedge funds have guaranteed some $14.5 trillion. (In a low-default environment, hedge funds would have viewed selling default swaps as free fee income.) Collateralization is spotty at best.

Analysts tend to pooh-pooh the scale of those numbers, and there is obviously some double-counting as market players buy protection to cover the guarantees they've sold. But unlike, say, futures exchanges, where all positions are netted each day, and cash margins are posted to cover any adverse changes, the "over-the-counter" markets in which default-swap contracts trade don't have such well-honed settlement arrangements. All settlements are counterparty to counterparty, so a sharp adverse change in markets could get very messy.

And just as with CDOs, the weakest link in the chain is the hedge funds. Credit hedge funds are reputed to account for about a third of total hedge fund equity, or some $750 billion, thought to be leveraged 5–10:1, and generally nearly fully deployed. Most funds could not survive even a 1 percent to 2 percent payoff demand on their default swap guarantees. Banks and investment banks are carrying large swathes of risky loans and investments at par because they have default insurance, but as the Bernstein analyst points out, their financial statements show no loss or bad debt reserves against the possibility of such failures.

Now consider how hedge fund counterparty defaults would rattle through the default swap markets. Large swathes of insured portfolios would have to be written down to reflect their intrinsic risk. The inevitable demand for collateral postings from the remaining insurance providers would withdraw huge sums from the credit markets, while the rush to extract cash from defaulting guarantors would trigger massive litigation. In short, we would be facing an utter thrombosis of the credit system that "could make the subprime mortgage problem look like a walk in the park." There is no point even in attempting to estimate the scale of the losses.

Hard Landing I: Recession

It has been fascinating to watch economic forecasters scramble to catch up to events through 2007. At the Federal Reserve's Congressional economic roundup in February, Chairman Bernanke portrayed what the *New York Times* called "a 'Goldilocks' economy that is neither too hot, with inflation, nor too cold, with rising unemployment." Even after the summertime Bear Stearns mortgage fiasco exposed the inherent fragility of structured finance markets, economists stuck with their sunny outlooks. Confidence was finally shaken only with the October–November rat-a-tat succession of big asset writedowns. As of late fall 2007, the case for a nasty recession was overwhelming.

Over the next two years, $350 billion in subprime and other risky residential mortgages will be reset, many at punishing rates. Defaults will rise sharply. A large number of people, perhaps as many as two million, could lose their homes.

House prices will continue to fall. Consensus estimates are for a real decline of 10 percent, but pessimists are expecting at least 30 percent—and pessimists have yet to be wrong in this cycle. Many consumers will be stuck with "upside-down" mortgages—i.e., greater than the market value of their homes.

Consumer spending *must* fall. Consumer spending jumped from a 1990s average of about 67 percent of GDP to 72 percent of GDP in early 2007. As Martin Feldstein, a former chairman of the Council of Economic Advisers, has pointed out, that increase was financed primarily by the withdrawal of $9 trillion in home equity and is no longer sustainable. Maintaining spending levels through the holiday season by running up credit card balances will just increase the severity of the subsequent crash.

Finished-goods exporters to America generally have swallowed the cost of the dollar's tumble, but that won't continue. Commodity exporters, however, are mostly passing through the dollar's decline, so the dollar prices of many raw materials, like oil, have been rising rapidly.

Exports will continue to improve and over time should make up for the fall in consumer spending. The shift from a consumer-driven to an export-driven economy should be a major factor in emerging from the recession a couple years from now. But it will be a wrenching shift and will take time.

A decline in credit availability, which is already apparent, will feed into the downward momentum. In November 2007, a Goldman Sachs analyst, Jan Hatzius, estimated that losses from subprime and related holdings at commercial banks would shrink bank capital by about $200 billion. At an average 10:1 ratio of lending to capital, that would trigger a credit withdrawal of about $2 trillion. Just in the month of November 2007, total market credit shrank by 9 percent, the biggest month-to-month drop on record. The credit shrinkage Hatzius projected would be several multiples larger.

A recent analysis of long-term leverage patterns at commercial and investment banks, in fact, suggests that the credit wind-down could be even more precipitate. Over an asset boom and bust cycle, commercial banks tend to preserve a roughly constant level of capital leverage—as capital dwindles, they contract credit provision at about the same ratio as they expanded on the way up. Investment banks, on the other hand, in part because of the way they manage their trading positions, tend to *increase* leverage ratios during an asset boom and *shrink* leverage ratios on the way down. Hedge funds follow the same pattern. Since hedge funds and investment banks now provide about half of all market credit, their accelerated deleveraging would make the total credit contraction far worse than in previous commercial-bank-driven cycles.

Hard Landing II: The Credit Meltdown

There is ample evidence that the Great Unwinding is already under way as this book goes into production, and it should continue through most of 2008. The first question is the likely economic losses due to defaults and writedowns. In November 2007, for the first time, mainstream analysts began to circle numbers that were much higher than previous ones and that finally were starting to make sense.

The table on the following two pages has my own estimates, which are higher still.

None of these is a stretch estimate, as the comments in the table suggest. As this book goes to press, Treasury secretary Henry Paulson is attempting to develop a program to mitigate the risks of residential mortgage defaults. Since it is likely that any such relief will be small, I do not factor it into the table. Finally, note that although many nondefaulted CDO and other risky bonds will recover to par as they approach repayment dates, I do not regard that as a recovery. The writedowns taken now are a measure of the yield the holder *should* be receiving for holding such a risky instrument, including the present value of principal repayment. Those losses occur over the life of the bond and are not restored when principal is repaid. The billions in writedowns being taken by banks certainly are real and have a profound effect on economic activity.

Although the table's numbers are daunting enough, the calculation assumes an *orderly* wind-down—as if all interested parties could agree on reasonable estimates of risk, take their writeoffs, and go about their business. So far, however, that has not been happening. The "super-SIV" structure floated by Citigroup and the Treasury looks like a blatant attempt to defer writedowns. The inconsistency of the market marks that have been taken so far also suggests considerable number juggling. Midquality subprime CDO tranches are carried at 90

Estimates of Defaults and Writedowns: Dollars in Billions (Updated for Paperback Edition)

INSTRUMENT	Current Outstandings	Default Percentage	Writedown Percentage	Recovery Rate	Net Loss
Residential Mortgages					
Subprime and other high-risk mortgage defaults	$1,500	30%	NA	50%	$225
Writedowns in nondefaulted SP-based CDO bonds*	$1,200	NA	40%	NA	$480
Writedowns in prime mortgages and prime mortgage ABS	$5,000	5%	NA	50%	$125
Subtotal					**$830**
Corporate Debt					
High-yield bond defaults	$1,000	10%	NA	50%	$50
High-yield bond nondefaulted writedowns	$900	NA	20%	NA	$180
Leveraged-loan CLO defaults	$500	20%	NA	50%	$50
Leveraged-loan CLO nondefaulted bond writedowns	$450	NA	30%	NA	$135
Leveraged-loans not in CLOs	$1,000	20%	NA	50%	$100
Subtotal					**$515**

* Outstandings = total current minus defaults

	Current Outstandings	Default Percentage	Writedown Percentage	Recovery Rate	Net Loss
Other Lending Sectors					
CMBS defaults	$950	10%	NA	50%	$48
CMBS nondefaulted bond writedowns	$855	NA	15%	NA	$128
Non-CMBS commercial real estate loans	$2,400	10%	NA	50%	$120
Credit Cards	$900	7.5%	NA	NA	$68
Auto loans	$800	25%	NA	60%	$120
Subtotal					**$484**
Credit default swap counterparty failures, including monoline insurers*	NA				$200
Grand Total					**$2,029**

*The amount here has probably already been realized. AIG holds $400 billion in unhedged CDS mostly with foreign banks that will require a payout of at least $150 billion. It will either be covered by the federal government's bailout or eaten by the foreign banks. (One can assume that it will be very hard to find out.) Monoline arrangements to unwind swaps in contemplation of default have cost their counterparties in the tens of billions, but again the numbers are very murky. There is no estimate of counterparty losses from the unwinding of hedge funds, which is just beginning to pick up speed as of this writing.

at the Swiss bank UBS and 63 at Merrill, while the ABX, a widely used index of such CDOs, trades at 40. Similar indexes on CMBS, leveraged loans, and credit default swaps all suggest that internal marks should be much higher.

The Center for Audit Quality, a professional standards group for certified public accountants, has issued a policy statement suggesting that current internal marking violates Financial Accounting Standards Board rules, which require the use of external "observable" data before resorting to in-house estimates. The center's statement specifically references the ABX as an example of observable market data. Banks presumably would not have to track the ABX precisely, but wide deviations probably would not be acceptable. (Since the indexes in question, like the ABX, are all created and managed by the major banks, they are in a poor position to argue their irrelevance.*) A quiet panic reportedly is building on Wall Street that their accountants will make them mark close to the available external indexes, which would require writedowns far greater than any seen so far. That situation will only be worsened by the current drive on the part of the ratings agencies to catch up to their huge backlog of overrated CDO debt.

---

*The indexes are run by a private London-based company, Markit. It has sixteen shareholder banks, including all of the biggest credit derivative and CDO dealer banks. The instruments and companies in each index are proposed by and voted on by the sixteen banks. The index for credit default swaps, for example, consists of swaps on 125 major companies, while the ABX index comprises twenty $500 million CDOs of subprime mortgages, in both cases chosen by the banks. Each index is tracked for five years, but a new version of each index is created, or "rolled," every six months.

Reflect back on the resolution of the LTCM crisis in 1998. Threatened with a possible global financial meltdown, Federal Reserve officials gathered twenty New York bankers in a conference room, and they agreed to put up $3.6 billion to resolve the crisis. In 2008, there is no one to call a meeting, there is no conference room big enough to hold the parties, and no one knows who should be on the invitation list.

The stage is set for a true shock-and-awe surge of asset writedowns through most of 2008. Widespread collateral defaults, particularly at the credit hedge funds, will trigger forced selling from margin accounts. Rolling downgrades will require divestitures by pension funds and insurance companies that find themselves in violation of rules on holding investment-grade paper. Holders of senior CDO tranches will liquidate their holdings as credit protection dissolves, as they have the right to do. Add in even mildly bad outcomes for the monolines and in the credit insurance markets, and the global financial system will be in catastrophe.

It amazes that we have come to such a place.

Minsky, Ponzi, and the Logic of Markets

Hyman Minsky was a Keynesian economist who became famous for his theory of financial crises. Unlike the Chicago-school free-market ideologues, Minsky believed that instability and crises were inherent features of financial markets. He posited a series of market stages, kicked off by some positive structural development, like the development of the junk bond–fueled takeover market in the 1980s, or the new credit technologies of the 2000s. Firms participating in the early stages of the cycle typically are not leveraged; Minsky called them hedged firms because their cash receipts cover their cash outlays. The success of the first movers draws in additional players, who inevitably engage in leverage to improve the yields earned by the cash players. Speculative firms then engage in leverage to the point where they must borrow to meet some of their interest payments—usually borrowing in short-term markets to finance higher-yielding long-term positions. None of this is irrational behavior; market players are chasing short-term gains, and some of them are getting very rich.

The final stages of a Minsky cycle arrive with a proliferation of Ponzi firms, which must borrow to meet all their interest payments, so their debt burden continuously increases. At some point, a disruptive event occurs, like the collapse of the United Airlines LBO in 1989, or the Russian bond default in 1998, and markets abruptly reprice—the further along in the cycle, the more violent the repricing.

Have we reached a Ponzi stage in the credit cycle? Ever since Paul Volcker put the inflation demons to flight in the early 1980s, *credit* has been the world's greatest growth market. World GDP has increased spectacularly over the past twenty-five years, but nothing like the explosion of credit. The total of global financial assets, which essentially are claims on GDP, was about the same as global GDP in the early 1980s. At the end of 2005, according to a recent International Monetary Fund analysis, global financial assets were about 3.7 times as high as global GDP. In other words, outstanding financial claims not only cover this year's GDP, but the next several years' as well. Financial derivatives, which represent claims on financial instruments, were a relatively rudimentary market in the 1980s. Their notional value by the end of 2005, however, was three times higher than the total of all financial instruments, and more than ten times higher than total global GDP. When those numbers are totted up for 2007, we undoubtedly will find that they have ratcheted up much higher still, with the upward curve tilting more toward the vertical.

It's worth unpacking the meaning of those numbers a bit. Financial claims, of course, are against assets, which are some multiple larger than annual GDP. Similarly, the notional value of a derivative refers not to the derivative but to the size of the portfolio it is referencing. But the enormous scale of outstanding financial claims and derivatives is a useful index of leverage in the world economy, and especially in the United States. Leverage, as we've seen, is the flip side of volatility. An option may be valued at, say, 5 percent of the portfolio it is referencing, but a small change in the portfolio value will cause very large changes in option values. With notional derivative values now in the $500 trillion range, rapid swings of $5 trillion to $10 trillion in derivative values are altogether plausible and could inflict enormous damage.

How could leverage get so high? In the class of instruments we've been talking about, there are relatively few "names," or underlying companies, that are deeply traded, several hundred at most. And a relatively small number of institutions, basically the global banks, investment banks, and credit hedge funds, do most of the trading. In effect, they've built a huge Yertle the Turtle–like unstable tower of debt by selling it back and forth *among themselves*, booking profits all along the way. That is the definition of a Ponzi game. So long as a free-money regime forestalled defaults, the tower might wobble, but stayed erect. But small disturbances in any part of the structure can bring the whole tower down, and the seismic rumblings already in evidence portend disturbances that are very large.

So that is the place where a quarter-century of Chicago-school piloting has brought us—to a debacle on at least the scale of the one caused by the liberal crackup of the 1970s.

The parallel with the 1970s is also important for how it was resolved. In one of the great episodes of American public service, Paul Volcker addressed the problems head-on, wrung inflation out of the economy, restored the international position of the dollar, and cleared the field for the economic booms of the 1980s and 1990s.

Contrast Volcker's behavior with that of the Japanese when their own asset bubble imploded in the late 1980s—a debacle also proportionally on the same scale as our current one, and much more like it in detail. There was no Japanese Volcker. Instead of addressing their problems, the tight network of incumbent politicians and bankers concealed them. And nearly twenty years later, Japan still has not recovered.

The American financial sector today is far more powerful than it was in the 1970s. And to date, its response to the looming crisis has been, overwhelmingly, to downplay and to conceal. That is a path to turning a painful debacle into a decades-long tragedy.

CHAPTER 7

Picking through the Shards

American workers give their all on the job, by any measure. They not only work longer hours than workers in any other advanced economy, but they also have the highest output per hour worked—with the sole exception of Norway's small workforce, who get credit for the country's huge output of oil.

Highest hourly output *and* longest hours! What an extraordinary resource. As the world's most valuable work force, they must surely be among the world's best paid and most coddled.

Well, not exactly.

Consider the tale of Travelport, a web-based reservations company. The Blackstone private equity firm and a smaller partner bought Travelport in August 2006. They paid $1 billion of their own money and used Travelport's balance sheet to borrow another $3.3 billion to complete the purchase. They doubtless paid themselves hefty investment banking fees, which would also have been billed to Travelport. After seven months, they laid off 841 workers, which, at a reasonable guess of $125,000 all-in cost per employee (salaries, benefits, space, phone, etc.), would represent annual savings of more than $100 million.

And then the two partners borrowed another $1.1 billion on Travelport's balance sheet, and paid that money to themselves, presumably as a reward for their hard work. In just seven months, that is, they got their $1 billion fund investment back, plus a markup, plus all those banking fees and annual management fees—and they still owned the company. And note that the annual $100 million in layoff savings would almost exactly cover the debt service on the $1.1 billion. That's elegant—what the financial press calls "creating value." Another word that springs to mind is "looting."

What Blackstone had done, of course, was to *reallocate* value, not create it. The sacked employees had possessed things of value, too—jobs and future earnings streams they thought were secure, health insurance, pension contributions. Taken together, the capitalized value of their jobs and benefits must have been about the same as the $1.1 billion owner's dividend that it was diverted to finance. There were also other costs, some of them not the kind that markets readily monetize. Many sacked employees, especially those in their fifties and sixties, were having trouble finding work, and many others were struggling without health insurance; the company was arguably worse off as well since it was saddled with more than $4 billion in debt. Add it all up, and value was destroyed, not created.

The private equity kings insist that they are management wizards, not financial engineers. But at least in its most recent phase, the numbers show that the private equity game, like subprime CDOs, is just another arbitrage on cheap money and rising asset markets. Researchers at the University of Pennsylvania's Wharton School have built a large database of private equity fund returns from reports furnished to clients. Fund partners earned twice as much money from transaction fees and fixed fund-management fees as they did from deal outcomes. The rewards, in other words, flowed to people who excelled at raising funds and executing deals, not to down-and-dirty turnaround specialists. For the highly evolved money-seeking organisms atop the buyout funds, spending time on anything other than window-dressing management would be irrational—especially when it's so easy to just take the cash.

The Ascent of Financial Services

Nine-figure compensation packages for bankers—and billion-dollar paydays for takeover artists and hedge fund managers—became routine in the 2000s. The Commerce Department measures the output of the financial sector in the 10–15 percent range of GDP, but finance captured more than 40 percent of all corporate profits at the peak of the credit boom.

In the previous chapters we've explored the primary instruments, the financing practices, and the technologies of the credit crisis, but in this section I'll try to summarize the macro developments that created such a *Hindenberg*-like bubble. Consider: Financial markets built an investment paradigm that applied high leverage to long-term illiquid instruments. Then compounded the danger by funding those instruments in the short-term debt markets. Then doubled the bet again by building the base portfolios from unusually risky securities, like subprime mortgages and leveraged loans. Then, finally, embraced a class of credit derivatives that ensured the swift propagation of any local collapse through the whole system. If a band of brainy terrorists had been hired to destroy Western finance, they could hardly have designed a more efficient assault.

How did it happen? The array of answers proposed below is necessarily tentative and impressionistic, although I think they are all relevant. The credit crunch is a landmark phenomenon in the history of finance that will be gnawed at by generations of academics. What follows is a list of topics that warrant gnawing.

The Rise of the Shadow Banking System.   One of the most striking developments of the past quarter century has been the migration of lending from relatively tightly regulated depositary banks to the capital markets. Capital market players, like investment banks and "mortgage banks," originate loans of all kinds and repackage them as securities to be placed with ultimate holders, such as pension funds and mutual funds. In principle, capital markets intermediation should, and often does, improve liquidity and lower borrowing costs—pension funds, for instance, are more suitable holders of residential mortgages than banks. In practice, lending in the shadow

banking system seems especially bubble-prone, in part because of the "Agency" problem—there is a wealth of evidence
that originators suspend credit vigilance when they're planning to sell off the loan. (Traders call it IBG-YBG lending—
"I'll be gone; you'll be gone.")

The High Leverage in Shadow Banking.   The "originate-and-
distribute" banking model can produce very high returns on
equity. Since loans are held only long enough to repackage
and sell them, they can be funded cheaply in the short-term
lending markets, and generate attractive fees when they're
sold. When times are good, the pressure is to build volumes
by increasing leverage. Financial-risk-based modeling abetted
the trend by obscuring true leverage at the big banks. In the
later stages of the crisis, the frenzied drive for ever higher
profits and bonuses compounded high leverage with high risk
instruments.

The Shift to Principal Transactions.   Traditional bankers,
both in commercial and investment banks, generally avoided
playing with the house's money. You made loans, took deposits, underwrote securities, and got paid for your work. All
banks had trading books—if you offered foreign exchange
services, you needed inventories of the major currencies. But
your trading was to support customers' business needs; the
wise bank treasurer kept his own books risk-neutral.

Goldman Sachs may have been the first to expressly shift
its emphasis to trading for its own account, but the move was
general by the mid–1990s. The soothing rain that watered
trading book profits, of course, was the steady fall in interest

rates engineered primarily by Alan Greenspan. For twenty-five years, on average, and with some bouncing around, the base interest rate fell about a third of a percent a year. Falling rates increase the value of fixed-income securities. Once the expectation of continuously falling rates was engrained in Wall Street's collective consciousness, banks built bigger and bigger trading books, even as the steady descent of rates pushed them to higher leverage and riskier instruments.

By year's end 2007, six big Wall Street banks had amassed a combined trading book of $2.1 trillion, up $519 billion in just one year. Their combined *negative* operating cash flow was $357 billion, which was a rough proxy for the funds they borrowed to grow their trading account and to pay cash bonuses on their mark-to-market profits.* The late Herb Stein's famous remark about unsustainable trends is a cliché because it's true. They tend to stop; and this one did.

Invisible Leverage. The stated leverage on balance sheets, including in the depositary banking system, typically misrepresented actual leverage. The misstatements were of two kinds. The first was to ignore "embedded" leverage. Consider an investment bank holding the "equity tranche" bonds on a

---

*The six were Citigroup, JP Morgan, Merrill, Lehman, Bear, and Goldman Sachs. Three of them, of course, no longer exist as independent entities. *The Economist* magazine recently attributed the shift to principal transactions to the "Big Bang" deregulation of brokerage fees, which eliminated a major source of banking profits. That may be true for the initial foray, but in a normal rate environment, leveraged own-account trading would have been much riskier, and banks would have been impelled to keep a much tighter rein on leverage and on the quality of the securities they were buying.

structured portfolio. The bonds would have a face value of, say, 3 percent of the total portfolio face, and be at risk for the first 3 percent of losses. The securities' embedded leverage would therefore be 33–1—so a 3 percent portfolio loss wipes out the entire tranche. But banks' asset books show all trading assets at their market value, without any reflection of embedded leverage, giving an inaccurate notion of likely volatility.

The second is the practice, now much reduced, of holding large portfolios off-balance-sheet in special purpose vehicles, like the notorious SIVs. My rough calculation is that in 2006, the true balance sheet exposure of JP Morgan Chase and Citigroup was about 150 percent bigger than their stated exposure. The accounting was perfectly legal. The guarantee to a SIV was priced as if the bank had sold a put option giving the SIV the right to sell back the portfolio at par. And how was the put option priced? By an internal model, of course, that assumed very low risk and volatility in the SIV, producing a trivial price that could be readily buried in "Other Liabilities." Technically, everything was fully accounted for.

The invisible leverage, of both the embedded and off-balance-sheet variety, was a major reason why asset unwinds were so violent and so startling, even to so many experienced, but evidently clueless, senior financial executives.

The New Monetarism.   The term is the coinage of David Roche, a British investment manager, and refers to the liquidity effects of the vast volume of outstanding financial derivatives. Buying and selling credit default swaps, for example, is now a standard proxy for buying and selling bond portfolios, and requires far less capital—in effect, the swaps increase the "money supply" available in financial markets. Securitization further amplifies market liquidity by converting more and more real assets into tradeable instruments—securitized home equity loans are futures on the unrealized capital gains in houses. But Roche points out that the new forms of money embodied in derivatives and securitized instruments can only be spent in financial markets; you can't use a CDO strip as currency. Roche may be on to something important: his "new money" is generally not captured by the Fed's standard monetary tracking indices and would tend to show up in asset bubbles rather than in consumer price inflation—all very consistent with recent events.

The Abdication of the Professions.   Post-mortems by Congress and regulatory bodies have fully exposed the complicity of the ratings agencies in the excessive valuations of high-risk instruments. A common, and disheartening, thread of the last couple decades' financial crises, from the Savings and Loan crash through Enron and the credit debacle, is the consistent failure of profit-making entities as statutory fiduciaries. The securities laws assume that lawyers, accountants, and credit raters will not allow monetary incentives to override their professional ethics—an assumption that draws little support from the abysmal recent record. It would be neither possible nor desirable to replace those certification functions within the public sector, but the current framework clearly needs some creative rethinking.

All of the causal factors cited so far are ones that played out in the financial sector rather than in the real economy. But there were ripplings between the financial sector and the real economy that conjure up parallels with the 1930s. A traditional, but now disfavored, explanation for the Depression is the trend, dating from the early 1900s, for corporate profits to rise faster than new investment, as the share of wages in national income fell. (The formation of U.S. Steel in 1902 pretty much ended the role of once powerful steel unions.) The consequence was a steady increase in the incomes of the wealthy, which, with the relative decline in investment, was naturally diverted into financial assets. To sustain the boom of the 1920s, markets invented new forms of consumer credit, including installment-buying and a widening market for home mortgages. As the consumer credit underlying the financial boom looked increasingly shaky, banks started packaging up their bad loans into highly leveraged "investment trusts" that they sold on the stock markets, feeding the equities bubble.

Yes, it does have a familiar ring. For the record, from 1980 through 2007, total employee compensation, including benefits, dropped from 60.1 percent of GDP to 56.3 percent; the ratio of investment to corporate profits was halved; and the share of GDP going to cash dividends nearly tripled. The government doesn't track the volume of stock buybacks, but they were also very high. The net effect was a huge buildup of investable cash that flowed toward the high returns available from risky consumer lending. And, indeed, the income share of the top tenth of the population rose to 49 percent, the highest share ever, a tiny fraction of a percent higher than in 1929. The Travelport story that opened the chapter fits right into this broader narrative. Wages and other payments to workers were converted to financial dividends that inevitably flowed to other financial assets—more company buyouts, hedge fund investments, and the like. Even Blackstone executives cannot possibly spend much of their vast incomes on goods.

I'll return to the questions of financial regulation and policy responses to the recession in the next chapter. First, I'd like to look a bit more closely at the question of income inequality.

Inequality

One of the most striking developments over the past quarter century is the dramatic shift of taxable incomes toward the wealthiest people. Between 1980 and 2006, the top tenth of the population's share of all taxable income went from 35 percent to 49 percent, an increase of about a third. The changing distribution *within* the top 10 percent, however, is what's truly remarkable. The unlucky folks in the ninetieth to the ninety-fifth percentiles actually lost a little ground, while those in the ninety-fifth to ninety-ninth gained a little. Overall, however, income shares in the ninetieth to ninety-ninth percentile population were basically flat (24 percent in 1980 and 26 percent in 2006).

Almost *all* the top tenth's share gains, in other words, went to the top 1 percent, or the top "centile," who more than doubled their share of national cash income from 9 percent to 20 percent. Even within the top centile, however, the distribution of gains was radically skewed. Nearly 60 percent of it went to the top *tenth* of 1 percent of the population, and more than a fourth of it to the top one-hundredth of 1 percent of the population. Overall, the top tenth of 1 percent more than tripled their share of cash income to about 9 percent, while the top *one-hundredth* of 1 percent—or fewer than 15,000 taxpayers—quadrupled their share to 3.8 percent of all taxable income. Among those 15,000, the average tax return reported $30 million of income in 2006, while the take for the entire group was $441 billion.

Conservatives have fiercely challenged these numbers on the grounds that the taxable incomes data does not include many government income transfers or investments in tax-deferred vehicles, like 401(k)s, which wealthier people have only limited access to. Those are true statements, but hardly change the data. Most transfers go to the elderly, and have been a major factor in lifting the elderly population out of poverty. Income transfers to the working-age poor, however, are relatively small, even including the Earned Income Tax Credit, and have little effect on the overall distribution of incomes. And while it's true that most of the investments of the wealthier classes are in taxable funds, they also have the lion's share of tax-deferred investments as well. The bottom three quintiles of earners have risibly small savings, including in tax-deferred accounts.

In any case, the argument about *whether* the past several decades have seen growing inequality in America was effectively closed by Federal Reserve chairman Ben S. Bernanke, a respected conservative economist, in a wide ranging speech delivered in February 2007. Reviewing all the evidence, Bernanke took the fact of growing inequality as settled, and challenged the economics profession to discover *why*.

Over the past ten years, in fact, academic economists have produced dozens of papers on the question. All of them confirm a steady widening of wage inequality that probably began in the 1960s and clearly accelerated in the 1980s. Increasing wage inequality, moreover, has been reinforced by a similar trend in benefits provision, especially with respect to healthcare and pensions, which consistently favor higher-paid workers. There is also good evidence that in the lower-skilled groups, incomes have become much less predictable; shakier job tenures play havoc with savings and trigger interruptions in basic benefits.

Explanations on the "why" of the growing disparity include, variously, the declining real value of the minimum wage, the globalization of work and the decline of unionism, the widening dispersion of education and other skill-differentiations within the labor force, and the effect of cheap computer power in enhancing the productivity of highly skilled people. That last point is worth emphasizing, for it suggests a compounding of effects—not only did the spread of post-college training increase skill disparities in the work force, but the internet and desktop computing power allowed the most skilled to accomplish more with their skills.

I will briefly unpack the arguments in one such analysis, not because it's the final word on the subject—I'm sure it's not—but because, of the dozen or so papers I've looked at, it strikes me as digging the deepest into the complexity of the data. The authors build a detailed database of job distribution, wages, and employee educational levels from 1963 through 2005, using a variety of Census and Labor Dept. monthly surveys. The data are not perfect, since collection methods were modified several times over the period, but they offer about as accurate a portrait as we are likely to get of the multi-decadal geologic shifts in the American job market.

The authors find that the trend toward greater dispersion of labor income by education dates from at least the 1960s, but with several distinct periodizations. After generally increasing during the 1960s, the income advantage of increased education actually dropped somewhat in the 1970s. The earnings gap particularly narrowed between college graduates and high school graduates. (Although the authors don't say so, the large wave of twenty-something boomer-generation college graduates entering the labor force in the 1970s must have pushed down the income premium commanded by a college degree.)

During the next period, from 1979 to 1987, the income advantage to education increased quite sharply in all tiers of the labor force. High school graduates widened their income advantage over high school dropouts, college graduates over high school graduates, and people with post-college degrees over college graduates. The falling real value of the minimum wage was an independent factor in the increased dispersion of lower-half incomes. The rapid decline of well-paid Rust Belt unionized jobs without educational requirements must have played a role as well.

The dispersion pattern shifted again through the 1990s and the 2000s—to what the authors call "polarized" trend lines. The 1980s collapse of incomes for the lowest tier workers stabilized in the 1990s—while they didn't improve their relative position, it stopped getting worse. For the middle tier, which includes workers with high school degrees, some college, or four-year college degrees, the income spread narrowed. In effect, college graduates without post-graduate training lost some of their advantage over people without college degrees. And finally, the top tier—those with post-college education—accelerated their ascent into the financial stratosphere.

The authors offer several hypotheses for those trends. At the bottom tier, the stabilization is probably explained by increased concentration of lower-tier workers in personal services occupations—orderlies, hair dressers, waiters—that are not easily automated. (The minimum wage was so low at this point that it was not a factor in the stabilization.) The compression in the middle, they hypothesize, is the consequence of automating tasks that college graduates were once required to perform, while the rising fortune of those at the very top is the inverse of the narrowing at the middle. As routine college-level work is automated, the people carrying out the highest order intellectual tasks capture more of the value for themselves.

I find that quite plausible. The advent of online databases and desktop computing power makes much of the old routines of digging, entering, and analyzing data unnecessary. Financial executives, especially those under fifty, can usually access all the data they need from their desktops and analyze it themselves, without the phalanxes of information workers, researchers, and financial report processors who used to pad out the middle layers of large companies. I also suspect that the rapid growth of the financial services industry is an independent, but related, factor. Financial services has accounted for a disproportionate share of corporate profits in recent years. The industry is a very efficient information processor, and while it pays well at all levels, top-level employees have done extraordinarily well. The national average income of stock brokers, for example, was $250,000 in 2005—although since active stock traders usually do less well than the overall market, brokers' economic contribution may be negative.

The implication of that analysis, and the many others like it, is that widening income dispersions may be a permanent feature of modern economies. But as the credit bubble, and Wall Street, implodes around us, it will be interesting to see whether the returns to graduate education regress to longer-term trends. I suspect they will somewhat, but not enough to erase the growing advantage at the top end.

Another recent study points to a second factor driving the post–1980 disparities: For the first time in American history, American native-born* educational attainment is not keeping pace with technological change. That is a radical break with a two-century American tradition. Thomas Jefferson helped found the University of Virginia, and can fairly be described as the first "education president." Almost all American states began investing heavily in free public education starting in the 1820s. At the height of the Civil War, Abraham Lincoln and the Republican Congress created the land-grant college system; it was the first time any government had imagined that higher education should be available to working people. The post-WWII GI Bill made America the world's first nation with a college-educated middle class. But in our generation, that proud legacy has been undercut by runaway educational cost increases, drying up of scholarship assistance

---

*The analysis focused on native-born to exclude any immigration effects.

except at the wealthiest universities, and transfer of most student assistance activities to profit-making entities like Sallie Mae. The privatized student lending sector has proven to be, in the main, grasping and unethical, suborning college tuition counselors and exploiting government subsidies to build the wealth of executives like Sallie Mae's Albert Lord—the Angelo Mozilo of student lending. As a nation, we should be embarrassed.

===

One of Anthony Trollope's greatest, and most sour, novels, *The Way We Live Now*, portrays the London of the 1870s when both society and government were in thrall to a rising new class of financial speculators. As it tracks the seeping corruptions, both petty and grand, that enmesh even the decent people, the novel takes on a melancholy, almost elegiac, air, as if Trollope had divined the passing of England's greatest days, when "British" stood for solid integrity and world-beating achievement. And in fact, within twenty years, the United States had equaled or surpassed Great Britain on virtually every economic measure, and its margin of superiority was widening by the day.

It's conceivable that America is now at just such a place. For most of the last decade, business and government have offered a depressing spectacle. The massive frauds of the Enrons and the WorldComs. The eager self-delusions and conscious deceits that underlay absurdly misrated CDOs. The shameless selling of the government, as epitomized by the Republican "K Street Project." The monetary helium from the Federal Reserve that fed asset bubbles, fueled a bread-and-circuses consumer binge, floated Wall Streeters into the financial stratosphere, and perhaps irrevocably debased the dollar.

A less apocalyptic reading is that we are witnessing the final days of another quarter-century political/ideological cycle—the last gaspings of the raw-market, Chicago-school brand of financial capitalism that moved into the vacuum created by the 1970s collapse of the Keynesian/liberal paradigm.

The great historian, Arthur M. Schlesinger, Sr., the father of the late historian and liberal pundit, may have been the first to suggest the existence of such cycles, and attributed them to a kind of Gresham's law of political motivation. Any shift of power in America requires building large coalitions, and the best people in the camps of both conservatives and liberals—or "radicals" in Schlesinger's terminology—"find themselves in bad company."

> The thinking conservative finds his chief allies in the self-complacency of comfortable mediocrity, in the apathy and stupidity of the toil-worn multitudes, and in the aggressive self-interest of the privileged classes.
>
> The honest radical draws much of his support from self-seeking demagogues and reckless experimenters, from people who want the world changed because they cannot get along in it as it is, from *poseurs* and *dilettanti*, and from malcontents who love disturbance for its own sake.

Political cycles turn after an extended period of either conservative or liberal hegemony bring the baser, more self-seeking, or barmiest, elements to the fore. The market and

regulatory reforms introduced by economic and monetary conservatives in the 1980s, I believe, made a major contribution to
the recovery of American competitiveness and economic
energy in the 1980s and 1990s. But as the more unsavory impulses in the conservative understanding have asserted themselves, the country has been brought to the brink of financial
and economic—and in the political realm, moral—disaster. All
the signs are that we are on the cusp of a turning of the cycle,
much like that in 1980, as evidenced by Barack Obama's and
the Democratic/liberal's sweep in the 2008 elections.

The new administration, however, is facing an exceedingly
nasty early agenda. The truly painful parts will be stripping
out the hundreds of billions of hokum on financial balance
sheets, shifting the real economy to a more sustainable, less
consumer-splurge-dependent basis, and reviving the dollar as
a serious currency. Although the challenges are different in
detail, the scale of the problem is much like that Paul Volcker
faced in 1979.

At some point, when we get through that, we will face a
long list of pressing problems that are, in effect, the detritus
left over by the passing of an old paradigm.

CHAPTER 8

Recovering Balance

In the 1990s, I had business relations with several Silicon Valley firms and often flew into San Francisco, rented a car, and drove south on Route 101. Once, for some reason, I drove down Route 1 instead, which runs along the ocean. I had never driven it before and was amazed at its beauty—the unspoiled dunes, the long beaches, the gorgeous mix of turquoises and earth tones. Then as the scene rolled on, mile after mile, I had a cognitive dissonance. "What's going on?! Where are the Arby's, the motels, the condos, the strip malls?" Then it dawned on me. "Oh, there used to be a *government* here."

California, in fact, for the first couple decades after WWII, under both Republican and Democratic leadership—Earl Warren, Goodwin Knight, and Edmund "Pat" Brown—set a new standard for high-quality local government. The great universities, the highways, the water system, the careful attention to environmental preservation, and much else that made

California such an attractive state (maybe *too* attractive) all date from that period.

Notwithstanding Chicago-school dogma—that government *is* the problem—it is often an important part of the solution. I make that statement in full awareness that even the fine California government eventually grew into such a state of bloat and inefficiency as to prompt an epoch-making taxpayer revolt—the famous Proposition 13 referendum in 1978. It was a signal episode in the unraveling of the old liberal Keynesian consensus, which was confirmed by the watershed election of 1980.

But now, after a quarter-century of chipping away at government, the domestic public sector in the United States has been impoverished and corrupted, and we're paying a price for it. Even as we dig out from our financial markets debacle, we will need to begin to restore some balance. The very first priority will be to restore effective oversight over the finance industry.

Financial Regulation

The figural sculptures on the facade of the New York Stock Exchange are titled *Integrity Protecting the Works of Man.* Investors might make a case for renaming them *Caveat Emptor.*

In the summer of 2007, Moody's, Standard and Poor's, and Fitch announced the first downgrades of triple-A and double-A CDO bonds collateralized by American residential mortgages. It was the opening flourish of what has become an endless parade of downgrades across the entire CDO and CLO markets. Recently issued paper with top-quality investment-grade ratings is routinely rerated as junk, usually causing mark-to-market losses of 20 percent, 30 percent, or even more. British money market funds, Arab sovereign investment programs, and German banks all have taken big financial hits. If the world loses confidence in American markets, the long-term costs will be far greater than a one-time trillion-plus balance-sheet writedown.

It is the transparency and integrity of American financial markets that has made them such a magnet for foreign investment, even at times like the present, when financial performance and the strength of the currency hardly justify it. That hard-won reputation was, to a great extent, the consequence of generally superb American markets regulation, epitomized by the SEC.

The American regulatory scheme is based on the insight that government can best support financial markets by ensuring that investors get accurate information. To manage the massive volume of American security issuance, the designers constructed a system that operates with a relatively small central staff, relying on the integrity of the accounting profession, the securities bar, and private rating agencies. After a quarter-century of antiregulatory zealotry, however, and a parade of fiascos from the S&L crash through the Enrons and WorldComs, and now the CDO mess, the credibility of that system, and with it the attractiveness of American markets, is at risk.

Only the most invincible dogmatists could survey the history of financial booms and busts and come away with the notion that markets are always right. But the confidence of even the truest believers might be shaken by the disastrous results of our latest experiment. There is no benevolent market genie behind the curtain, diligently ensuring least-squares approximations to efficient frontiers—just the usual motley of sharks, decent people, charlatans, and some serious intellectuals, mostly playing with other people's money.

———

Herewith, after a year of tracking the unfolding of the crisis, is a partial agenda for re-regulating finance.

Above all, be careful.　　There have been a number of instances over the past year when spastic regulatory twitches arguably acted as crisis accelerants. The SEC's ban on stock short-selling is an example. By disrupting hedging strategies at big investment funds, the ban may have triggered forced unwinding and panic-inducing stock selloffs. The unwind was necessary, of course, but might have been accomplished more smoothly and gradually in the absence of the ban.

The regulatory failures, in any case, were preponderantly failures of *supervision*, rather than failures of regulatory design. Yes, there are holes in the system, but the Federal Reserve, the Comptroller of the Currency, and the Securities and Exchange Commission had an abundance of actual and implied powers to cut off the worst of the credit fiascos before they reached the danger point. (Notice the rich menu of unsuspected powers that the Fed and the Treasury have discovered now that banks are losing money.) The real problem was that our regulators and their industries both worshiped at the same shrine of efficient markets. Intervention was against their religion.

Finally, the most attractive, the simplest, and the stupidest regulatory response is to rearrange boxes on organization charts. The creation of the Department of Homeland Security is a cautionary example, and the financial regulatory blueprint offered by treasury secretary Paulson springs from the same impulse. The important challenge is to decide what regulations are *for*, and to let the structure flow from that.

Focus on leverage.   A root cause of the credit crisis was the shift over the early 2000s to the new "Basel II" system of calculating leverage through model-based "value at risk" (VAR) analyses. "Basel I," established by global agreement, was in reaction to the banking excesses of the 1980s. It imposed a fairly simple-minded, but effective, risk-adjusted 8:1 leverage limit on all depositary banks. In the United States, Basel I lined up well with a long-standing SEC limit of 15:1 leverage for broker-dealers. Both were replaced by the ostensibly more sophisticated Basel II rules in 2004. On my sample of large bank balance sheets, gross leverage quickly increased by about 50 percent, not including the concealed leverage in off-balance-sheet vehicles.

The failure of VAR has been cataclysmic. While it may be a useful tool for balance sheet analysis, regulatory thresholds should shift back to much simpler—more visible—numerical standards. Model-based regulation is far more elegant, of course, but trillions in losses are a big price for elegance.

Just as important, bank balance sheets must be utterly transparent. Everything with any retained risk should be on the balance sheet, including contingent liabilities, like guarantees. Their greater transparency is the prime attraction of "covered bonds," a quasi-securitization technique espoused by Paulson. A bank issues bonds secured by specific assets, like residential mortgages, which reduces borrowing costs, but the entire liability remains a general obligation of the issuer.

Transparency, finally, must penetrate beyond nominal balance sheet asset values to the embedded leverage in the asset. Heavy capital charges should apply to loans to highly leveraged entities, or against highly leveraged assets. (Even Alan Greenspan imposed such a rule in the late 1980s.)

Concentrate regulation on depositary banks.   It is not possible to regulate hedge funds and private equity funds effectively—they can domicile in Madagascar if they choose—so it is probably wiser not to try. The important object is to wall them off from the depositary banks and the payments system. Currently, federally-insured depositary banks are major providers of prime brokerage services, including margin lending, to hedge funds and similar entities. That creates an infection vector for converting hedge fund excesses into systemic risk. Restrictions on bank lending to highly leveraged entities would close off those infection channels. We'll also need limits on the size of non-regulated entities, to head off the "too big to fail" syndrome. (An "entity" should be defined by control parties rather than legal structure.) Assets of "X" should trigger intrusive regulation, but no access to Fed lending. If the payment system is safe, the government shouldn't care how rich people invest their money.

Once the depositary banks are walled off from high-risk enterprises, the regulatory challenge is simple. Banking should be dull. Credit analysis should dominate over financial engineering. Trading functions should be in support of customer services. Well established OTC instruments like interest rate and currency swaps are appropriate for hedging balance sheet exposures; but trading in immature instruments, like credit default swaps, should be limited to exchange-traded, standardized, paper.

Boring banks also happen to be quite profitable. RBC (former Royal Bank of Canada) and TD Bank (former Toronto-Dominion) have turned in excellent profits and high equity returns throughout the 2000s, greatly outperforming their brilliant and swashbuckling American cousins. An RBC executive I spoke to recently said, in effect, "We looked at all those CDOs and other structured instruments and decided that they just weren't what we did." In other words, bankers can be successful again, if they just go back to being banks—and there's nothing mysterious about regulating banks.

Beware the universal bank.   Many observers have hailed the voluntary conversion of the last free-standing investment banks—Morgan Stanley and Goldman Sachs—into Federal Reserve member banks. It's supposed to signal a new era of tighter regulation and lower leverage. I don't believe it for a minute. It's almost certainly a ploy to gain more entitled access to the Fed's balance sheet without changing basic businesses. Three-quarters of Goldman's 2007 pretax profits came from Principal Transactions. Betting the store is what they do, and they're not going to jettison their primary business.

The universal bank is a bad idea. While it may be too late to kill it, regulators will have to concentrate hard on creating internal walls. My pessimistic guess is that they won't succeed.

Protect the asset shares of the depositary banks. While the shift of assets to the shadow banking system seems to follow a smooth curve, if one looks at the annual net new lending shares of each sector, they jump around quite a lot. The loss of share by depositary banks usually follows a crisis—so there was a big loss in the early 1980s, when banks were struggling with bad petrodollar loans, and again in the late 1980s, in the wake of big losses on LBOs and commercial real estate. The regulatory response was usually to suspend accounting rules and infuse liquidity. But that favors expansion of the shadow banks, since they react faster to liquidity infusions. A different strategy would be to re-equitize the depositary banks in place of a general liquidity increase. A supporting tactic would be for the Fed to engineer surprise rate increases from time to time, to prevent the shadow banks from becoming too comfortable about piling on the leverage.*

---

*The only "anti-punchbowl" interest rate rise during Alan Greenspan's tenure as Fed chairman was in February 1994, which caused the crash in the CMO market discussed in Chapter 3. The verbatim transcripts of that and subsequent Fed meetings are voluminous, and I may have missed something, but I cannot find a single reference to CMOs. It appears the rate increase was based on a general feeling that the economy was getting too frothy, and the CMO bubble just happened to fall out of the trees. (Even after the event, no one mentioned it, as if they didn't notice, although there was clear awareness that markets had been quite rattled.) Intended or not, popping the CMO bubble resulted in a ten year successful run for conservatively structured CMOs—until they were swept away in the subprime lunacy.

Create a fiduciary structure around the government's private-sector interventions. Now that the government is taking ownership positions in many private companies, it is time to regularize the process. The major interventions so far, as in Bear and AIG, have been rushed, inconsistently priced, and poorly documented. It's essential that standing working panels be established, ideally including highly regarded professionals, to establish pricing rules, to review and approve terms on individual deals, and to create audit trails of the negotiations. It may take a little longer, but the randomness of the current process creates serious reputational and financial risk.

Further, the security holdings created by such transactions should not be at the disposal of either the Congress or any member of the executive branch. Depositing the securities in the Social Security Trust Funds, under the supervision of an independent board of directors with fiduciary obligation to the beneficiaries of the Trusts (like independent directors of mutual funds), would greatly reduce the possibility of political manipulation in the management of the portfolios.

If we are somehow successful in reining in the destructive impulses of the big banks, we will make credit more expensive, perhaps take a few tenths of a percent off GDP growth, and make banking a lot less fun. But finance is not supposed to be a casino.

Achieving Recovery

I have already described why I believe a serious recession is inevitable, and probably even desirable. The credit-fueled, consumer-driven economy of 2002 through 2007 is just not sustainable. The government response to date—which seems concentrated on getting back to way things worked in 2006—is doomed to failure, while the oceans of money thrown at the banking system to "restore liquidity" could have severe unintended consequences. The necessary transition is from a credit-driven, consumer-based economy to one characterized by higher savings, higher investment, and less import-dependence. The scale of that shift is so large that I doubt that it can be navigated without a major recession.

I don't pretend to know how to restart healthy, self-generating growth, but two areas warrant attention.

Infrastructure.   Infrastructure ranks high on everyone's list. We have serious shortfalls in public goods—like highways, transportation and airports, sewer and water systems in older cities, and perhaps most important, our outdated and jury-rigged electrical grid. Infrastructure also plays to industrial sectors, like large-scale project management and heavy equipment, where Americans have substantial competitive advantage. The challenge is how, in an overleveraged country, to raise the debt to cover such huge investment.

The solution may be to privatize the infrastructure build, and finance it through Sovereign Wealth Funds. Long-term American bonds secured by toll charges may be an attractive way for them to monetize their store of Treasuries, and would help put the offshore dollar overhang to work in America. The returns required would likely be higher than those on the Funds' current stocks of Treasuries, but locking in long-term liabilities now would protect against the steep Treasury yield curve that could follow a disorderly overseas dollar diversification. (It hasn't happened yet, I know, but it is still very likely. There are recent reports of meetings between Chinese and Japanese finance officials to discuss joint strategies for limiting their heavy dollar risk.)*

Infrastructure might also provide an avenue for revising our relationship with China in mutually beneficial ways. China will be very hard hit by the American consumer downturn, but also has one of the world's worst infrastructure deficits. Use of its dollar balances for infrastructure would create important export opportunities for American companies as well as new employment opportunities in the Chinese interior. (Large-scale agricultural operations, another American specialty, may offer additional cooperative opportunities.)

Health Care.   My second, and last, example is health care. I will treat it at greater length because it's big, controversial, and I think badly misunderstood by mainstream analysts.

Free-market conservatives have long campaigned to make health care much more of a "marketized" industry; unfortunately, it's beginning to look like a caricature of our automobile industry—specializing in SUVs and Hummers, because that's where the margins are.

Advanced procedure by advanced procedure, American medicine is the best in the world. But we make a dreadful

---

*Privatized infrastructure investment is not without complications. Road tolls sufficient to remunerate private bond holders, some studies suggest, may drive truck traffic onto the free highways, creating large additional maintenance requirements. Road tolls therefore may have to be subsidized to maintain optimum balances. Serious attention to the electrical grid may require a reorganization of the regulation and ownership structure of the grid.

hash of the low-margin, boring things that can pay large dividends in the medium and longer term, like perinatal care and care management for the very expensive patients with multiple chronic diseases.

The rising pressure to cut health care spending almost for its own sake is misplaced. Health care is one of the most dynamic and innovative sectors of the economy. It is an important driver of both electronics and biotechnology, and a positive contributor to America's current account problems. It is also a generally good employer that pays above-average wages and offers a growing variety of professional and semi-professional careers—as physicians' and surgeons' assistants, imaging technicians, inhalation therapists, and many more.

Economic theory, in fact, suggests that health care *should* be expanding rapidly. The richer you get, the more you are likely to favor life-extending spending over additional consumption. The extra enjoyment from one more toy, in other words, can't begin to match up against an extra year of life to enjoy all of your toys. Even at moderate-to-low rates of economic growth, there is no reason why the economy couldn't support the expansion of health care to 25 percent to 30 percent of GDP, as I expect will happen by 2030 or so. Even at that level, we can still carry on consuming more housing and electronic toys from Asia, if not at quite the same pace as before.

But having said all that, American health care is also extremely wasteful and is an operational mess. At twice the per capita level of spending as in other advanced countries, we are not getting a good deal. Much of the problem stems from the insistence that health care is just like any other consumer market. It's not.

In normal markets, competitors who roll out new products the fastest usually win. The most advanced sectors of the American health care system behave that way, rolling out new technologies much faster than anywhere else, but it's *not* a good thing. The introduction of cardiac stents in the 1990s and 2000s is a good example. (Stents are tiny mesh scaffoldings that prop open blocked arteries.) Super-rapid adoption of the newest stent classes in the United States ran well ahead of outcomes data, necessitating forced pullbacks to more appropriate patient populations as data came in. Other countries adopted more cautiously and built up to stable usage rates close to where the Americans eventually settled on the way down. America's high-speed technology adoption cycles produce higher financial returns for drug companies, device makers, and aggressive medical practitioners, but often it is not good medicine and is very expensive. A related phenomenon is the clear preference for high-reimbursement treatments regardless of their real advantages over equally effective, lower-cost alternatives.

Secondly, and shockingly for a country that leads the world in the application of computer technologies, America is dead last among advanced countries in the application of computers to health care management. American primary care doctors are the least likely to have electronic record-keeping systems, and among the least likely to be able to order a prescription electronically or to access a patient's test results or hospital records. If health care were a normal market, a half-dozen big companies would have long since hired all the doctors, put the small groups out of business, and built big data systems and data exchanges. But it's not that kind of market, so government has to take the lead.

Finally, the traditional American payroll-based system of financing health care is clearly breaking down. As the GDP share of health care keeps rising, the lower half of the payroll market can't afford it, and workers can't pay the premiums on their own. Although health care is not a right in the legal sense, all advanced countries except the United States have defined a standard health care package as an important element in a decent standard of living. Given the vast accretions of national wealth over the past couple decades, it is disgraceful that we still fall short of that norm.

I won't speculate on possible solutions, but they will inevitably involve an expansion of government. We should stop fighting ideological battles over whether government should have any role and start concentrating on how to make it effective and efficient.

Others might come up with different priority lists—like education and energy efficiency—but most of them will require shoring up the public sector, and some, like health care, will entail substantial tax increases. And that will require coming face-to-face with the past quarter-century's ruling ideology that expanding public resources is always wrong.

The Limits of Markets

It is a canon of Chicago-school economics that government resource allocations always reduce productivity. As a blanket proposition, that's evidently wrong. The federal government lavished a great deal of money on the semiconductor industry and the Internet, for example, and we're clearly much better off for it. Since the beginning of the republic, public works investments—canals, railroads, highways, airports—have generally paid high returns. In the nineteenth century, a British parliamentary commission identified America's greater investment in public education as a major competitive advantage. Government spending, in short, is productive or not, depending on what it's spent on.

But there is substantive truth behind the detestation of public spending. It is that any privileged industry—and public enterprises are prone to become privileged—will eventually fatten to the point where it becomes a drag on, or even a threat to, the health of the economy. But that's a general argument about privilege, whether it arises from tax subventions or some other source. The financial meltdown chronicled in this book was to a great extent the consequence of coddling our financial industry, fertilizing it with free money, propping it up with unusual tax advantages for fund partners, and anointing it with fresh funds whenever it stumbled or scraped a knee.

The real premise of the Chicago-school argument for shrinking the public sector is the much shakier one that free markets always achieve the best outcomes. That claim, however, presupposes that economists can identify best outcomes. Market economists typically use the standard of Pareto optimality. (Vilfredo Pareto was a famous nineteenth-century economist.) A distribution such that no group member could be made better off without making someone else worse off is

Pareto-optimal. The problem is that there are always many possible Pareto-optimal outcomes, most of them not very attractive. A society where everyone has equal wealth is Pareto-optimal, but so is a society where one person has half of everything and everybody else has equal shares. In both cases, no one could be made better off without making someone else worse off.

Ever since Pareto, some of the world's greatest economists have tackled the distribution problem and have produced many interesting ways of framing the issues. But no one has come up with much that is of practical use. The data are intractable, analytic results are often self-contradictory, and even believers in the quest concede that the models make sense only in perfect markets, which is no place where people live. The fallback among free-market economists, therefore, is usually to adopt a total output measure, like GDP growth or national productivity, as a best-outcome proxy. But that reduces competitions among social systems to the principle that the country with the most toys wins, which is ridiculous.

Many of our current problems stem from the fact that our financial markets are super-efficient at financing bigger houses, bigger cars, and toys from Asia—but not much else. France has had lower economic growth than the United States for a number of years, even though hourly output per worker is roughly the same—it was a hair behind America's in the last competitive survey and was a hair ahead in the previous one. The French middle classes have smaller houses and cars than their American peers, but better diets, considerably more leisure time, and much more economic security, while the distance between the top and the middle is not nearly so wide as here. France is hardly a perfect country. Its unions and public sectors seem much too privileged, and racial issues are becoming much more intractable. But all in all, a lot of Americans, especially those who are not on top of the food chain, might think it's a pretty good trade.

In other words, it comes down to taste, and balance, and judgment. My personal belief is that the 1980s shift from a government-centric style of economic management toward a more markets-driven one was a critical factor in the American economic recovery of the 1980s and 1990s. But the breadth of the current financial crash suggests that we've reached the point where it is market dogmatism that has become the problem, rather than the solution. And after a quarter-century run, it's time for the pendulum to swing in the other direction.

NOTES

Unless otherwise indicated, all U.S. economic data are from official government sources.

Chapter 1: The Death of Liberalism

For Elbert Gary and American steel competitiveness, see Kenneth Warren, *Big Steel, The First Century of the United States Steel Corporation, 1901–2001* (Pittsburgh, PA: University of Pittsburgh Press, 2001), 32–50 and 249–58. The quote on lowering prices is from Mark Ruetter, *Sparrows Point and the Rise and Ruin of American Industrial Might* (Urbana, IL: University of Illinois Press, 2004), 395. The Galbraith quote is from John Kenneth Galbraith, *The Affluent Society* (Boston, MA: Houghton Mifflin, 1958), 351. The phrase "managerial capitalism" is Alfred D. Chandler's. See his *Scale and Scope, The Dynamics of Industrial Capitalism* (Cambridge, MA: Harvard University Press, 1990.) For the 1960s mergers, see my *The Coming Global Boom* (New York: 1990), 64–5. For Pinto and Vega, Dan Lienert, "The Worst Cars of All Time," *Forbes*, January 27, 2004.

The demographics discussion follows Richard Easterlin, *Birth and Fortune: The Impact of Numbers on Personal Welfare* (New York: Basic Books, 1980). The Herbert Stein quote is in Robert L. Bartley, *The Seven Fat Years and How to Do It Again* (New York: The Free Press, 1992), 27, which is a good, detailed, if partisan, history of the economics of the era. Gold prices are from Global Financial Data. The quote on Carter's anti-inflation program is from the *New York Times,* May 26, 1979. The Romney and Burns quotes are in Bartley, *Seven Fat Years,* 29, 27. The Tyson quotes are from John Zysman and Laura Tyson, eds., *American Industry in International Competition: Government Policies and Corporate Strategies* (Ithaca, NY: Cornell University Press, 1983), 5, 7. The quote on Japan is from William S. Dietrich, *In the Shadow of the Rising Sun: The Political Roots of American Economic Decline* (University Park, PA: Pennsylvania State University Press, 1991), 247. For the MIT studies, see the MIT Commission on Industrial Productivity, *The Working Papers of the MIT Commission on Industrial Productivity* (Cambridge, MA: The MIT Press, 1989). For Japan and IBM, see Charles H. Ferguson and Charles R. Morris, *Computer Wars* (New York: Times Books, 1993). The Grove quote is from an interview with Ferguson and me during the *Computer Wars* research. For Friedman's extreme views on deregulation, see Milton and Rose Friedman, *Free to Choose: A Personal Statement* (New York: Harvest Books, 1990), 207–10 for drug regulation.

Chapter 2: Wall Street Finds Religion

Frank Knight's quote is from Johan Van Overtveldt, *The Chicago School* (Chicago: Agate Press, 2007), 67. The James Stewart quotes are from his *Den of Thieves* (New York: Touchstone, 1992), 17–18. Bartley on Steiger and venture capital is from Robert L. Bartley, *Seven Fat Years,* 61, 143–44. For a discussion of taxes and venture investing, see Paul A. Gompers and Josh Lerner, "What Drives Venture Capital Fund Raising?" *Working Paper 6906,* National Bureau of Economic Research, January 1999. On oil price decontrols, the *Times* quotes are from Robert D. Hershey, "Why Gasoline Is Getting Cheaper," April 12, 1981, and Douglas Martin, "Economic Gains Tied to Ending Oil Price Curbs," September 8, 1981. U.S. energy efficiency data are from U.S. Department of Energy, "Energy Intensity Indicators," http://intensityindicators.pnl.gov/total_highlights.stm, updated through June 1, 2006. The calculations of structural versus efficiency gains start only in 1980. The downsizing of energy-intense industries appears to have accelerated considerably in the 1980s, however, in part because the new openness to market outcomes facilitated the cleaning out of a lot of industrial dead weight. For the non-U.S. data, "Primary Energy Supply per Unit of GDP" (table), *Energy Balances of OECD Countries, 2003–2004* (Paris, France: International Energy Agency, 2006), II 333.

William Greider's *The Secrets of the Temple: How the Federal Reserve Runs the Country* (New York: Simon & Schuster, 1987) is an indispensable history of the early 1980s battle against inflation, although Greider's Populist perspective threads throughout the book and often skews his judgments. For "candidate of Wall Street," 47. For the Fed's war on inflation, I use both Greider and the *New York Times* for context, but the substantive account, including the struggle to adhere to monetarist principles, is drawn almost entirely from the transcripts of the Federal Open Market Committee meetings, which are available from the Federal Reserve's Web site, www.federalreserve.gov. The transcripts are from tape recordings of the meetings, which have been lightly edited for intelligibility but not reviewed by the participants and which also include the technical staff appendices. They are made available with a five-year time lag. Greider did not have access to the transcripts; at the time he wrote his book, Alan Greenspan insisted that they had all been destroyed. Volcker's "certainly some . . ." is from an interview; ". . . hullaboo," FOMC transcript, October 6, 1979, 8–9. "Verdun" editorial, *New York Times*, October 14, 1979. "Even from the labor," FOMC transcript, May 20, 1980, 17. Volcker's "If we let up," Greider, *Secrets of the Temple*, 465.

The standard sources for the LBO boom are James Stewart, *Den of Thieves*, and Connie Bruck, *The Predators' Ball: The Inside Story of Drexel Burnham and the Rise of the Junk Bond Raiders* (New York: Penguin, 1989). I have a chapter-long account in my *Money, Greed, and Risk* (New York: Times Books, 1999). I was a valuation consultant to several buyout funds during this period. *Money, Greed, and Risk* also has an extended analysis of the S&L crisis, with extensive sources. There are no final numbers on the total cost to the government. The bad S&Ls were wound up so quickly, and their books were in such disarray, according to FDIC staff I spoke to in 1998, that they gave up any attempt to tot up a final accounting.

For the struggle over Clinton's first budget, see Bob Woodward's day-by-day account, *The Agenda: Inside the Clinton White House* (New York: Simon and Schuster, 1994). Greenspan's "irrational exuberance" quote was on December 5, 1996. See David Leonhardt, "Remembering a Classic Investment Theory," *New York Times*, August 15, 2007. For the "new paradigm," "Greenspan and His Friends," *Time*, November 10, 1997. For Rubinomics, Glenn Hubbard, "The Contradictions at the Heart of Rubinomics," *Financial*

Times, November 18, 2003. I've also heard Rubin make those claims in speeches at policy conferences. For empirical data on deficits and interest rates, see "Long-Term Effects of Chronically Large Federal Deficits," Congressional Budget Office, October 13, 2005. The analysts cite a number of reasons why deficits are bad for the country, but higher interest rates isn't one of them. The average of multiple studies is that running a deficit of 1 percent of GDP for ten years would raise long-term interest rates by 30 basis points (three-tenths of a percentage point). That result shouldn't be surprising: Additional U.S. debt is sold into a $40 trillion or so global market. An extra couple hundred billion is noise level. For deficits and inflation, Chryssi Giannitsarou and Andre Scott, "Inflation Implications of Rising Government Debt," *Working Paper No. 1264*, National Bureau of Economic Research, October 2006, suggesting only "extremely modest" interactions. The factors driving toward a 1990s boom were set out in my "The Coming Global Boom," *Atlantic Monthly*, October 1989, based primarily on the work of Ed Yardeni, then chief economist of Prudential-Bache.

Chapter 3: Bubble Land: Practice Runs

I wrote extended analyses of the first two episodes in this chapter in *Money, Greed, and Risk*, 184–205, 140–50, and 158–64. The current Vranos fund status is from the *Financial Times*, October 10, 2007. For the LTCM episode, I rely primarily on Roger Lowenstein's fine account, *When Genius Failed: The Rise and Fall of Long-Term Capital Management* (New York: Random House, 2000). The "eat like . . ." quote and Mayer's question on the "real scandal" are from Martin Mayer, *The Fed* (New York: The Free Press, 2001), 267–68. The four Greenspan quotes are from: Lowenstein, *When Genius Failed*, 106; testimony before the House Committee on Banking and Financial Services, September 16, 1998; remarks to the Chicago Conference on Bank Structure and Competition, May 8, 2003; and testimony before the Committee on Banking and Financial Services, October 1, 1998. The Countrywide example is from Gretchen Morgenson, "Inside the Countrywide Lending Spree," *New York Times*, August 26, 2007. Fischer Black wrote a number of pieces on the shortcomings of Black-Scholes, e.g., "How to Use the Holes in Black-Scholes," *Journal of Applied Corporate Finance*, Winter 1989, 78–83. At a number of places in his LTCM book, however, Lowenstein suggests that Merton, in particular, thought that the mathematics captured something like Truth. The Merrill Lynch executive is Dan Napoli, who was a source for *Money, Greed, and Risk*. The quote is from an interview. Napoli was fired after the LTCM scandal, in which Merrill lost heavily. It was a clear case of scapegoating. The LTCM lending account was managed by the most senior executives at the firm, who bypassed all of Napoli's risk-management systems.

Chapter 4: A Wall of Money

My thanks to Nouriel Roubini for free access to the Roubini Global Economic Monitor (RGE Monitor), a massive collection of up-to-date documentation on current credit and economic issues. The "thirty-one-month" figure was cited by Robert Shiller at an on-the-record symposium at the Council on Foreign Relations, September 11, 2007. (Using the CPI, I calculated an even longer period.) Further Shiller statements in this section and the Burns-Greenspan comparison are from the same symposium. The Greenspan "new credit paradigm" quote is from a speech to the American Bankers Association, October 5, 2004. Banker's "wall of" and "chasing" are from the *Wall Street Journal*, November 3, 2005. William McChesney Martin's "punch bowl" quote is from Martin Mayer, *The Fed*, 165. The narrative of the Fed's rate actions follow the minutes of the FOMC, available at www.federalreserve.gov. The *Economist*'s "the global" quote is from "The Disappearing Dollar," December 2, 2004. The Roach "unconscionable" quote is from the CFR symposium. The "Asset Price Bubbles and Monetary Policy" study is from the *ECB Monthly Bulletin*, April 2005, 47–60; quotes from 53–4. The investment letter is *Facts & Trends, Gary D. Halbert's Weekly E-Letter*, August 28, 2007.

The Merrill housing data are from "A Home-Grown Problem," *Economist*, September 10, 2005. For housing prices and inflation, see Dean Baker, "Midsummer Meltdown: Prospects for the Stock and Housing Markets," Center for Economic and Policy Research, August 2007, 8. There are multiple indices for measuring housing prices. Dimitri B. Papadimitrou et al., "The Effects of a Declining Housing Market on the U.S. Economy," *Working Paper 506*, Levy Economics Institute of Bard College, July 2007, uses different indices from Baker's but comes up with virtually identical numbers.

The sources for the narrative of the housing bubble, besides those cited above, include: Faten Sabry and Thomas Schopflocher, "The Subprime

Meltdown: A Primer," NERA Economic Consulting, June 2007; Joseph R. Mason and Joshua Rosner, "How Resilient Are Mortgage-Backed Securities to Collateralized Debt Obligation Market Disruptions?" (preliminary), presented at Hudson Institute, February 15, 2007; and John B. Taylor, "Housing and Monetary Policy," presented at the Federal Reserve symposium on Housing, Housing Finance, and Monetary Policy, Jackson Hole, Wyoming, September 2007. For the interplay between housing finance and consumer spending, see Alan Greenspan and James Kennedy, "Sources and Uses of Equity Extraction from Housing," Federal Reserve Board, 2007; Christian Menegatti and Nouriel Roubini, "The Direct Link between Housing and Consumption: Wealth Effect and Home Equity Withdrawal," RGE Monitor, September 2007; and Karen E. Dynan and Donald L. Kohn, "The Rise in Household Indebtedness: Causes and Consequences," Federal Reserve Board, August 8, 2007. For a rich compendium of lending abuses, see testimony of Michael D. Calhoun, president, Center on Responsible Lending, "Calculated Risk: Assessing Nontraditional Mortgage Products," testimony before Senate Committee on Banking, Housing, and Urban Affairs, September 20, 2006. Mozilo's complaint is in Gretchen Morgenson and Geraldine Fabrikant, "Countrywide's Chief Salesman and Defender," *New York Times*, November 11, 2007. Jordan's story and the recent record of the industry in New York, including foreclosure maps, were provided by Sarah Ludwig of the Neighborhood Development Advocacy Project and Meghan Faux of South Brooklyn Legal Services. Faux recently made a detailed presentation of abuses to the New York State Assembly. For the affluent and subprimes, "The United States of Subprime," *Wall Street Journal*, October 10, 2007. And see "Briefing: America's Economy, Getting Worried Downtown," *Economist*, November 23, 2007, for a report on the growing pessimism.

Satyajit Das, *Credit Derivatives, CDOs, and Structured Credit Products* (New York: Wiley Finance, 2005), is a comprehensive text on the more arcane instruments. The notional value of credit default swaps is from the semi-annual surveys of the International Swaps and Derivatives Association (ISDA). For leveraged loans and subprimes in CDOs, see, for example, "CDO Spotlight: Is Fortune for Structured Finance CDOs Tied to RMBS Performance for Better or Worse?" Standard & Poor's, September 7, 2005 (on why CDO managers prefer subprime), and "CDO Spotlight: The Covenant Lite Juggernaut Is Raising CLO Risks—And Standard & Poor's Is Responding." For synthetic CDOs, "Structured Credit Special Report, Synthetic Overview for CMBS Investors," Derivative Fitch, June 6, 2007, and

"Synthetic CDOs, the Next Level," Global Legal Group, January 2006. Challenges in agency modeling are explored in great detail in "CDO Spotlight: Update to General Cash Flow Analytics Criteria for CDO Securitizations," Standard & Poor's, October 17, 2006. For ABCP, see "Asset-Backed Commercial Paper & Global Banks Exposure—10 Key Questions," Fitch Ratings special report, September 10, 2007. Massive amounts of reports and research are available on all aspects of securitization from all three rating agencies—S&P, Moody's, and Fitch. Most are available to the public. S&P also publishes regular roundups and market size estimates. Mason and Rosner, "How Resilient," also have a good discussion of the embedded leverage in MBS CDOs. The Tavakoli example is from the footnote on p. 26. Paul J. Davies, "Sales of Risky 'Synthetic' CDOs Boom," *Financial Times*, February 12, 2007, contains a range of quasi-official estimates of market size. My account of the Bear Stearns and ABCP events are drawn from numerous articles in the financial press. For the Rhinebridge liquidation, Neil Unmack, "Rhinebridge Commercial Paper SIV May Not Repay Debt," Bloomberg, October 18, 2007. The "buyer's strike" quote is from Gillian Tett, "Investors in Commercial Paper Go On Strike," *Financial Times*, September 10, 2007. For the growing chaos in the SIV markets, Paul J. Davies, "Banks Bear Strain of Short-Term Debt Market Troubles" and "SIVs Face Fight to Survive, Says Moody's," and Gillian Tett, "Superfunds Struggle to Take Off," *Financial Times*, November 15, November 9, and October 25, 2007, respectively.

Chapter 5: A Tsunami of Dollars

The more important studies and reports I used in the analysis of America's trade and investment position include: Ben S. Bernanke, "The Global Savings Glut and the U.S. Current Account Deficit," Federal Reserve, March 10, 2005; and "Global Imbalances: Recent Developments and Prospects," Federal Reserve, September 11, 2007; Maurice Obstfeld and Kenneth Rogoff, "The Unsustainable Current Account Position Revisited," *Working Paper 10869*, NBER, October 2004; "Oil-Exporting Countries: Key Structural Features, Economic Developments, and Oil Revenue Recycling," *ECB Monthly Bulletin*, July 2007, 75–86; Michael Dooley and Peter Garber, "Is It 1958 or 1968? Three Notes on the Longevity of the Revived Bretton Woods System," June 2005 (unpublished version from RGE Monitor); Nouriel Roubini, "The Instability of the Bretton Woods 2 Regime," July 2007 (unpublished version from RGE Monitor); Barry Eichengreen, "Global Imbalances and the Lessons of Bretton Woods," *Working Paper 10497*, NBER, May 2004; Joshua Aizenman, "Large Hoarding of International Reserves and the Emerging Global Economic Architecture," paper presented at the Growth and Business Cycles Conference, University of Manchester, July 12–13, 2007; Stephen Jen, "The Biggest Dollar Diversifiers Are American," Morgan Stanley Global Economic Forum, July 20, 2007; and "China Quarterly Update," World Bank Office—Beijing, May 2007. The *Economist*'s "biggest default" is from the issue of November 17–23, 2007.

For the details of individual country surpluses and sovereign wealth funds, the more important sources included "Remarks by Undersecretary for International Affairs Clay Lowery on Sovereign Wealth and the International Financial System," U.S. Department of the Treasury, June 2007; Stephen Jen, "How Big Could Sovereign Wealth Funds Be by 2015?" Morgan Stanley Global Economic Forum, May 4, 2007; "China's New Sovereign Wealth Fund: Implications for Global Asset Markets," *Insights*, Henderson Global Investors, Edition 14–17, July 2007; Brad Setser and Rachel Ziemba, "What Do We Know About the Size and Composition of Oil Investment Funds?" RGE Monitor, April 2007; "Sovereign Wealth Funds: The New Bogeyman of International Finance?" Economist Intelligence Unit, July 4, 2007; Esther Pan, "Backgrounder: China, Africa, and Oil," Council on Foreign Relations, January 26, 2007; Serhan Cevick, "The Challenging Trail of the Weaker Dollar," Morgan Stanley Global Economic Forum, September 20, 2007; Ramin Toloui, "Petrodollars, Asset Prices, and the Global Financial System," *Capital Perspectives*, PIMCO, January 2007; Caroline Newhouse-Cohen, "Japan's Balance of Payments," BNP Paribas, July 2007; and "Managing Japan's Foreign Reserves," *Japan Times*, August 3, 2007. Bernanke's 2004 paper is Ben S. Bernanke, Vincent R. Reinhart, and Brian P. Sack, "Monetary Policy Alternatives at the Zero Bound: An Empirical Assessment," Staff Working Paper, Federal Reserve Board, 2004–48. The Fed balance sheet data are from the weekly H4 reports.

Chapter 6: The Great Unwinding

Sources for the role of hedge funds in structured finance include Fitch Ratings, special report: "Hedge Funds: An Emerging Force in the Global Credit Markets," July 18, 2005; special report: "Hedge Funds: The Credit

Market's New Paradigm," June 5, 2007; "Assigning Credit Ratings to Hedge Funds," April 17, 2007; Asset-Backed Special Report: "Midyear 2006 Term ABS Recap and Outlook," July 26, 2006; Asset-Backed Special Report: "Term ABS Credit Action Report: August 2007"; "Credit Derivatives Update," March 6, 2007; and special report: "CDX Survey—Market Volumes Continue Growing while New Concerns Emerge," July 16, 2007. Also Derivative Fitch, Structured Credit Special Action Report: "CDO Asset Management in a Time of Illiquidity," September 21, 2007; Benedikt Goderis et al., "Bank Behavior with Access to Credit Risk Transfer Markets," Center Discussion Paper ISSN 0924–7815, Tilburg University, October 2006; Günter Frank and Jan Pieter Krahnen, "Default Risk Sharing between Banks and Markets: The Contribution of Collateralized Debt Obligations," *Working Paper 11741*, NBER, November 2005; Adam B. Ashcraft and João A. C. Santos, "Has the Credit Default Swap Market Lowered the Cost of Corporate Debt?" Federal Reserve Bank of New York, Staff Report No. 290, July 2007. The Fitch prime broker survey was in "Hedge Funds: The New Credit Paradigm." The two quotes are from pp. 7, 5. The Deloitte valuation practice survey is "Precautions That Pay Off: Risk Management and Valuation Practices in the Global Hedge Fund Industry." The report is (oddly) not dated, but reports on a survey conducted in the summer of 2006. Inter–hedge fund trading to prop up nominal prices is from Susan Pulliam et al., "U.S. Investors Face an Age of Murky Pricing," *Wall Street Journal*, October 12, 2007. Markit Inc. has published extensive materials backing up its indices. My thanks to Teresa Chick and Gavan Nolan at the company for detailed explanations and backup material, and for confirming details of the operations of the ABX indices. Reports on Bear, Merrill, and current markets are all drawn from the financial press.

For high-yield market development and default rates, Edward I. Altman, "Global Debt Markets in 2007: New Paradigm or the Great Credit Bubble?" *Journal of Applied Corporate Finance* 19, no. 3 (Summer 2007): 17–31; "U.S. Ratings Distribution: A Twenty-Five-Year March to Junk," Standard & Poor's Global Fixed Income Research, November 2006; Martin Fridson, "Could Default Rates Escalate Rapidly?" *Distressed Debt Investor,* Fall 2006; "U.S. Financing Gap: Long-Term Gloom Not Short-Term Stress," J. P. Morgan Chase, Economic Research Note, September 21, 2007; Bank of America Business Capital, "How Second-Lien Lenders Might Fare When Bankruptcies Increase"; "Why Due Diligence May Be Getting Short Shrift"; "Why the Use of Covenant-Lite Loans Is Growing in Europe," all from *CapitalEyes*

(July/August 2007); "Loan Issuance Boom Shifts Refinancing Risk Strongly to the Loan Market," Fitch Ratings, July 26, 2007; "High-Yield and Leveraged Loan Market Review, Second Quarter 2007," August 27, 2007; Henny Sender, "Banks Grease the Leveraged Loan Machine," *Wall Street Journal*, October 10, 2007; and James Mackintosh, "Banks Use Discounts to Tempt 'Vulture Funds,'" *Financial Times*, October 4, 2007. My thanks to William Ackman, chairman of the hedge fund Pershing Square Capital, for furnishing me an investors' conference presentation, "Who's Holding the Bag?" (May 2007) (unpublished). For the economics of private equity, Andrew Metrick and Ayako Yasuda, "The Economics of Private Equity Funds," University of Pennsylvania, Wharton School, Department of Finance, September 9, 2007. The Financial Services Authority report is "Discussion Paper: Private Equity, A Discussion of Risk and Regulatory Engagement" (November 2006); the quotes are from 64–66. The Greenspan quote is from a speech of May 16, 2006, provided to me by Satyajit Das. For credit cards, Peter Gumble, "The $915 Billion Bomb in Consumers' Wallets," *Fortune*, November 1, 2007, and statement of Sheila C. Bair, chairman FDIC, "Improving Credit Card Consumer Protection," U.S. House of Representatives, Financial Services Committee, June 7, 2007.

I also found the broader perspectives in the following papers to be quite useful: Michael D. Bordo, "The Crisis of 2007: The Same Old Story, Only the Players Have Changed," remarks, Federal Reserve Bank of Chicago and International Monetary Fund Conference: Globalization and Systemic Risk, September 28, 2007; Claudio E. V. Borio, "Change and Constancy in the Financial System: Implications for Financial Distress and Policy," *Working Paper No. 237*, BIS, October 2007; and IMF, Chapter 2: "Do Market Risk Management Techniques Amplify Systemic Risks?" *Global Financial Stability Report*, September 2007, 52–76. Finally, Joseph R. Mason and Joshua Rosner, "Where Did the Risk Go? How Misapplied Bond Ratings Cause Mortgage-Backed Securities and Collateralized Debt Obligation Market Disruptions" (in draft), is an important contribution to understanding the egregious failings of the ratings agencies with this class of instruments.

The Bernanke "Goldilocks" quote is from the *New York Times*, February 14, 2007. For a new note of pessimism, see Martin S. Feldstein, "Housing, Credit Markets, and the Business Cycle," *Working Paper No. 13471*, NBER, October 2007. Also, Christian Menegatti and Nouriel Roubini, "The Direct Link Between Housing and Consumption: Wealth Effect and the Home

Equity Withdrawal," RGE Monitor, April 2007. In addition to the sources cited in the notes to Chapter 4, there is also a useful collection of conference papers from the October 11, 2007, American Enterprise Institute Conference, "Deflating the Housing Bubble II," which are available at www.aei.org. The cited forecasts are mostly from the financial press, and I have tried to keep them as current as possible as the book goes to press. For the different leverage patterns among commercial and investment banks, Tobias Adrian and Hyun Song Shin, "Liquidity and Leverage" (September 2007), originally presented at the Sixth BIS Annual Conference, "Financial Systems and Macroeconomic Resilience," June 18–19, 2007. CMBS data are from *Commercial Mortgage Alert*, the industry bible. See especially the issue of November 16, 2007. For monolines, Gillian Tett, "Downgrade Fears Dog Monolines," *Financial Times*, November 8, 2007, is a good summary. The analysis of the credit default swap market follows Ted Seides, CFA, "The Next Dominos: Junk Bond and Counterparty Risk," originally in Peter Bernstein's *Economics and Portfolio Strategy* newsletter, reproduced in John Mauldin's *Outside the Box* newsletter, November 26, 2007. All the data in my loss estimate tables are sourced elsewhere in the book. For the Center on Audit Quality, see "Measurements of Fair Value in Illiquid (or Less Liquid) Markets," October 3, 2007, available from the center.

For Hyman Minsky, Martin H. Wolfson, "Minsky's Theory of Financial Crises in a Global Context," *Journal of Economic Issues*, June 1, 2002. The leverage discussion here follows closely a panel presentation by Andrew Sheng at the Tenth Annual International Banking Conference, Federal Reserve Bank of Chicago, September 27–28, 2007. The data on financial assets and derivatives are from the Statistical Appendices to the "Global Financial Stability Report," IMF, April 2007. I also benefited greatly from discussions with Satyajit Das, who has shared a number of his presentations.

Chapter 7: Picking through the Shards

The productivity data were compiled by the United Nations' International Labor Organization; see, e.g., CNNMoney.com, "U.S. Workers: World's Most Productive," September 3, 2007. The Travelport story is from Ianthe Jeanne Dugan, "How a Blackstone Deal Shook Up a Work Force," *Wall Street Journal*, July 27, 2007. For the nature of private equity returns, Andrew Metrick and Ayako Yasuda, "The Economics of Private Equity

Funds," University of Pennsylvania, Wharton School, Department of Finance, September 9, 2007. The paper was also widely reported in the financial press—e.g., Tracey Tennille, "It's the Fees, Not the Profits," *Wall Street Journal*, September 13, 2007.

The data on principal transactions are drawn from bank financial reports. See David Roche and Bob McKee, *New Monetarism* (London: Independent Strategy, 2007). The real-economy parallelisms between the current period and the Depression are pointed out by James Livingston, "The Great Depression and Ours," Parts I and II, posted by Mark Thoma, http://economistsview .typepad.com/economistsview/2008/10/income-shares-a.html. The data analysis from the current period is mine.

The tax data are from Emmanuel Saez and Thomas Piketty, "Income Inequality in the United States, 1913–1998," originally published in the *Quarterly Journal of Economics* 118, no. 1 (2003): 1–39. Tables and figures updated to 2005, downloadable in Excel format from http://elsa.berkeley .edu/~saez. The segment calculations are mine. These data include income from capital gains (which makes surprisingly little difference). For Alan Reynolds's view, see his "The Truth about the Top 1%," *Wall Street Journal*, October 25, 2007. The Bernanke speech is Ben S. Bernanke, "Speech before the Greater Omaha Chamber of Commerce, Omaha, Nebraska," Federal Reserve System, February 6, 2007. The paper I follow in the text is David Autor, Lawrence Katz, and Melissa Kearney, "Trends in U.S. Wage Inequality: Revising the Revisionists," NBER, March 2007. Other useful papers included: Claudia Goldin and Lawrence F. Katz, "Long-Run Changes in the U.S. Wage Structure: Narrowing, Widening, Polarizing," *Working Paper No. 13568*, NBER, November 2007; Ian Dew-Becker and Robert J. Gordon, "Where Did the Productivity Growth Go? Inflation Dynamics and the Distribution of Income," *Working Paper No. 11842*, NBER, December 2005 (which highlights the outsize gains of rock-star CEOs and hedge fund managers); Wojciech Kopczuk et al., "Uncovering the American Dream: Inequality and Mobility in Social Security Earnings Data Since 1937," *Working Paper No. 13345*, NBER, August 2007 (a long-term study that finds a sharp rise in inequality after 1970; it also finds that increased earnings mobility for women in recent decades masks a significant decline in earnings mobility for men); Flavio Cunha and James J. Heckerman, "The Evolution of Inequality, Heterogeneity and Uncertainty in Labor Earnings in the U.S. Economy," *Working Paper No. 13526*, NBER, October 2007 (documents the rise in earnings uncertainty among lower-income groups). For the Sallie Mae story, see

David Cay Johnston, *Free Lunch: How the Wealthiest Americans Enrich Themselves at Government Expense (And Stick You with the Bill)* (New York: Portfolio, 2007), pp. 151–157. (My appreciation to Johnston for sharing a galley of his book. Page citations in the final publication may differ.) The Schlesinger quote is from Arthur M. Schlesinger Jr., "Arthur M. Schlesinger Sr.: *New Viewpoints in American History* Revisited," *New England Quarterly* 61, no. 4 (December 1988), 483–501, at p. 500.

Chapter 8: Recovering Balance

For early downgrade notices, see "S&P Correct: Global CDO Deals Exposed to Subprime RMBS Reviewed," July 10, 2007. For a thoughtful, comprehensive analysis of the steadily increasing risk in American banking over the past generation, see Arthur E. Wilmarth Jr., "The Transformation of the U.S. Financial Services Industry, 1975–2000: Competition, Consolidation, and Increased Risk," *University of Illinois Law Review* 2002: no. 2, 216–476. The section on health care policy follows closely the "Policy" chapter in my recent *The Surgeons: Life and Death in a Top Heart Center* (New York: Norton, 2007). For an excellent analysis of the stent rollout, see "Drug-Eluting Stents: A Paradigm Shift in the Medical Device Industry," *Case OIT–50*, Stanford Graduate School of Business, February 13, 2006.

INDEX

Jennifer E. Morris

CHARLES R. MORRIS has written ten books, including *The Cost of Good Intentions*, one of the *New York Times'* Best Books of 1980, *The Coming Global Boom,* a *New York Times* Notable Book of 1990, and *The Tycoons,* a *Barrons'* Best Book of 2005. A lawyer and former banker, Mr. Morris's articles and reviews have appeared in many publications including *The Atlantic Monthly,* the *New York Times,* and the *Wall Street Journal.*

PublicAffairs is a publishing house founded in 1997. It is a tribute to the standards, values, and flair of three persons who have served as mentors to countless reporters, writers, editors, and book people of all kinds, including me.

I. F. STONE, proprietor of *I. F. Stone's Weekly*, combined a commitment to the First Amendment with entrepreneurial zeal and reporting skill and became one of the great independent journalists in American history. At the age of eighty, Izzy published *The Trial of Socrates*, which was a national bestseller. He wrote the book after he taught himself ancient Greek.

BENJAMIN C. BRADLEE was for nearly thirty years the charismatic editorial leader of *The Washington Post*. It was Ben who gave the *Post* the range and courage to pursue such historic issues as Watergate. He supported his reporters with a tenacity that made them fearless and it is no accident that so many became authors of influential, best-selling books.

ROBERT L. BERNSTEIN, the chief executive of Random House for more than a quarter century, guided one of the nation's premier publishing houses. Bob was personally responsible for many books of political dissent and argument that challenged tyranny around the globe. He is also the founder and longtime chair of Human Rights Watch, one of the most respected human rights organizations in the world.

. . .

For fifty years, the banner of Public Affairs Press was carried by its owner Morris B. Schnapper, who published Gandhi, Nasser, Toynbee, Truman, and about 1,500 other authors. In 1983, Schnapper was described by *The Washington Post* as "a redoubtable gadfly." His legacy will endure in the books to come.

Peter Osnos, *Founder and Editor-at-Large*